"And Prairie Dogs

Jewish Women in the Upper Midwest Since 1855

Linda Mack Schloff

MINNESOTA HISTORICAL SOCIETY PRESS
St. Paul

"And Prairie Dogs Weren't Kosher"

Weren't Kosher"

The publication of this book was made possible in part by a generous grant from
THE LUCIUS N. LITTAUER FOUNDATION.

This book is associated with a major exhibition and education project undertaken by the Minnesota Historical Society and the Jewish Historical Society of the Upper Midwest on the history of Jewish women in the Upper Midwest. We gratefully acknowledge the following major donors for their generous support of this project.

Lead Sponsor
NATIONAL ENDOWMENT FOR THE HUMANITIES

Major Sponsors
THE PAULA AND WILLIAM BERNSTEIN FOUNDATION
THE NATHAN CUMMINGS FOUNDATION
JEWISH COMMUNITY FOUNDATION
    MINNEAPOLIS FEDERATION FOR JEWISH SERVICE
THE JAY AND ROSE PHILLIPS FAMILY FOUNDATION
SHARRON L. AND OREN J. STEINFELDT

Sponsors
LYLE AND JANIS BERMAN
NATHAN M. AND THERESA BERMAN
THE FITERMAN FAMILY
N. BUD AND BEVERLY GROSSMAN FOUNDATION

HARRY KAY FOUNDATION
DEERA AND ALBERT TYCHMAN
UNITED JEWISH FUND AND COUNCIL
    THE JEWISH FEDERATION OF GREATER ST. PAUL

Title page: North Dakota homesteader Bessie Schwartz (left) and several members of her family outside her sod hut, about 1890

Minnesota Historical Society Press
St. Paul 55102

Manufactured in the United States of America
10 9 8 7 6 5 4 3 2 1
International Standard Book Number 0-87351-337-1 (cloth)
                0-87351-338-X (paper)

∞ The paper used in this publication meets the minimum requirements of the American National Standard for Information Sciences—Permanence for Printed Library Materials, ANSI Z39.48-1984.

Library of Congress Cataloging-in-Publication Data
Schloff, Linda Mack
    And prairie dogs weren't kosher : Jewish women in the upper Midwest since 1855 / Linda Mack Schloff.
    p. cm.
  Includes bibliographical references and index.
    ISBN 0-87351-337-1. — ISBN 0-87351-338-X (pbk.)
    1. Jews—Middle West—Social life and customs. 2. Jewish women—Middle West—Social life and customs. 3. Jews—Middle West—Biography. 4. Jewish women—Middle West—Biography. 5. Middle West—Ethnic relations. I. Title.
F358.2.J5S35 1996
305.48'8924024—dc20   96-8853

Contents

Preface and Acknowledgments

This book has its origins in an exhibition, *Unpacking on the Prairie: Jewish Women in the Upper Midwest*, which was organized by the Jewish Historical Society of the Upper Midwest and the Minnesota Historical Society and opened in October 1996. Research for the exhibition turned up a trove of compelling first-person accounts and photographs from a phase of Jewish settlement in America that had been sparsely documented. It quickly became clear that only a fraction of that rich material could be incorporated in the exhibition and that important themes could only briefly be explored. Also, the exhibition would only last so long. A book, on the other hand, would both make a fuller historical treatment possible and allow for a more effective use of the many wonderful personal stories and reflections that were at the heart of the project. This publication, then, is intended as a legacy of sorts from one Jewish generation to another. It is my hope that readers will be moved to learn still more about the ordinary yet remarkable people who made a Jewish life for themselves in the Upper Midwest.

I recognize the need to equip this particular legacy with a few notes of explanation. For a start, transliterating from Yiddish and Hebrew is a notoriously difficult, often downright anarchic, business. I found that a surprisingly large number of words from both languages appear in the unabridged *Webster's Third New International Dictionary*—and hence have entered the English lexicon. Thus in this book they are printed in regular type. In *Webster's*, the guttural-sounding Hebrew letter *het* is rendered with a *ch*, as in

Chanukah. For those words that remain in italics, I relied on trans-literations that are common in scholarly literature. However, I have retained original spellings within quoted passages even when they vary from those employed in the text.

The English spoken and written by many of the people quoted here is far from faultless. Nevertheless, I have respected their syntax and diction in order to preserve the flavor of their speech. There are two exceptions to this rule. First, I found it necessary to edit the oral histories in order to rid them of many stops and starts that characterize spoken accounts and that would have made reading them more difficult. Second, I rearranged three very long quotes in order to present the reader with more linear stories. These are: the tale of Fannie Goldfine's prowess as a businesswoman in Duluth (pages 140–42), which was spliced from two sources—a family history and a personal letter; Myer Shark's oral account of High Holiday services at the Devils Lake, North Dakota, courthouse (page 179); and Rabbi Julie Gordon's oral account of a triple bat mitzvah in Albert Lea, Minnesota (page 188).

Wherever possible, I have included women's first, maiden, and married names. I wanted to remind readers that women's individual identities remain connected to their birth families even when they formally join the families of their husbands. In instances where the words are those of a child or young unmarried woman, I used maiden names only.

·

Many institutions and individuals helped bring the exhibition and this book to life. In 1992 the Minnesota Humanities Commission and the Women's Endowment Fund of the Minneapolis Federation for Jewish Service provided seed money for research efforts. Two years later, the National Endowment for the Humanities provided a planning grant; this enabled me to explore the collections of the American Jewish Archives in Cincinnati and to visit Jewish communities in Sioux Falls and Aberdeen, South Dakota. Also in 1994, a number of volunteers from the Twin Cities Jewish community combed local oral history collections and written accounts, searching for authentic voices to tell the story of settlement in and adaptation to the Upper Midwest. They succeeded magnificently, and to them I owe quite a debt. The sources for all the written and oral materials recorded in this book are listed in the bibliography.

I am also indebted to the various institutions and people who gave their permission to be quoted or to use photos in their possession. In some cases, it proved impossible to trace donors; I hope they or their heirs will contact me.

I am immensely grateful to The Lucius N. Littauer Foundation for its contribution to the funding of this book, as I am to the other donors listed on the copyright page.

Marilyn Chiat, Riv Ellen Prell, and Rudolph J. Vecoli of the University of Minnesota gave sound advice at every stage of exhibition planning and development. Judith Shendar, also of the University of Minnesota, worked with me (under various titles) to create the exhibition; she was both a source of information and a superb sounding board. Both as an exhibition advisor and through her own writings, Jenna Weisman Joselit of Princeton University shaped my views on the development of American-Jewish material culture. Professors William Sherman, University of North Dakota, and J. Sanford Rikoon, University of Missouri, generously shared with me the fruits of their research on Jewish farmers. Kevin Proffitt, archivist at the American Jewish Archives, Freda Hosen of Sioux Falls, and Bea Premack and Gail Pickus of Aberdeen all provided vital assistance. Sandra Abramson, Barbara Cohen, and Margery Weisman helped me probe the 1910 United States manuscript census and tabulate findings. My heartfelt thanks go as well to the other twenty-odd volunteers and student interns—you know who you are!—who worked alongside me.

My son Aaron sharpened my prose and thinking, as did my rigorous and knowledgeable editor at the Minnesota Historical Society Press, Phil Freshman. I am grateful as well to the several academic reviewers who read various drafts of the manuscript. Assistant editor Deborah Swanson tenaciously checked sources and created the bibliography. She, in turn, was aided by Richard Hedrick, Hebrew Union College, Cincinnati; Pat Maus, administrator, North-east Minnesota Historical Center, University of Minnesota, Duluth; Joanne M. Sher, independent researcher; and again, Kevin Proffitt.

Finally, my husband, Leonard, enthusiastically encouraged me in my work at each of the countless steps along the way—even when it meant the loss of a bicycling companion. This volume is dedicated to him.

L. M. S.

# INTRODUCTION

ZLOTA RIVKA SVIDELSKY was a rather typical turn-of-the-century Eastern European Jewish immigrant. In 1903, at age forty, she left the Ukrainian town of Zhitomir with her husband and seven children. Perhaps the least typical portion of her family's journey was their destination: St. Paul, Minnesota. Upon arrival, they settled on the West Side, an area then favored by immigrant Jews. The community was no larger than ten square blocks, but it contained synagogues, a mikvah (ritual bath), kosher butcher shops, and, by 1911, a Hebrew school called the West Side Hebrew Institute. These were all necessities in Zlota Rivka's life.

She had a large family, but her responsibilities encompassed more than caring solely for them and maintaining a kosher home. She was the *zogerke* (most learned woman) in her synagogue. Sabbath and holidays would find her in the women's balcony, guiding her friends through the prayer service. Zlota Rivka also worked outside the home for income. She swept up and maintained the Hakhnoses Orkhim, which consisted of several rooms at the Hebrew school set aside for housing Jewish wayfarers. Yet there was more. She founded the Women's Free Loan Society so that Jewish immigrant women like her would have the money for the rudimentary furniture they needed to set up housekeeping on this side of the ocean.

Family and keeping kosher, work, synagogue, and organizations that aided community members—these were intersecting spheres, and within each she had obligations. This is what her culture had taught her. Once transplanted to St. Paul she began the process of re-creating, as best she could, her roles within the realms of her ethnicity and her religion.

Zlota Rivka Svidelsky (second from left) and her family in a photograph probably taken in Russia before 1903, the year they immigrated to America

This book is about women like Zlota Rivka. It uses the voices of four generations of Jewish women who settled in the Upper Midwest—Minnesota, North and South Dakota, parts of Iowa, and northern Wisconsin—to show how Jewish women transported, maintained, and transformed those four spheres of Jewish life in a region inhabited by relatively few Jews. The comments of men on the activities and the tribulations of their mothers, wives, and sisters have been included as well. In some cases, male voices are the only ones available in the historical record to illustrate important points. In some cases, too, their words prove to be illuminating in ways that are exceptionally vivid.

"*And Prairie Dogs Weren't Kosher*" explores two themes. The first is how Jewish women, immigrating to the region either directly from abroad or from other parts of the United States, helped settle and adapt to life on the prairies and in the small towns and cities. This book relates how they created Jewish homes, found jobs predicated either on Old World skills or Upper Midwestern opportunities, and preserved and established Jewish institutions and organizations. The first three chapters, which focus on the Old World background and on settling in new environments, enlarge upon this theme, as do the first parts of the chapters on work (Chapter Four), synagogues (Chapter Five), and organizations (Chapter Six).

The second theme of the book is how Upper Midwestern Jewish women created new roles for themselves outside their homes that were consonant with becoming middle-class Jewish Americans. Here, specific regional flavor becomes subsumed under national Jewish trends. This is particularly evident in the chapters dealing with women's work for organizations and synagogues, which serve to carry the story into the 1990s.

Although most of the voices heard in this book come from the period between 1890 and 1920, there are several reasons for extending the time line up to our own day. One reason is that Jewish women's organizational life did not really begin flourishing until the 1920s; it reached its peak as late as the 1950s. Another reason is that the stamp of ethnic identity did not fade away with the virtual end of immigration in the 1920s. Historian Andrew R. Heinze, in his book *Adapting to Abundance* (1990), described how Jewish women between 1880 and 1914 laid the foundation for a Jewish-American identity in part through their role as consumers. Consumerism continued to be an indicator of ethnic redefinition in the ensuing decades. For instance, starting as early as the mid-1920s, Upper Midwestern Jewish women began buying Chanukah decorations for their homes and presents for their children, both of which practices represented a break from the way that holiday had been celebrated in the past. Objects made in Palestine could be found in the homes of Zionists beginning in the 1930s. One can argue that by the late 1940s, when Jewish women began buying Israeli-made objects from synagogue gift shops, modifications of ethnic identity had become evident. True, women were supporting the manufacturing sector of the newly created state. In another sense, though, they were trading in their European ghetto identity for that of the victorious Israelis.

Still another reason to take the story to the present day is that, just as ethnicity has continued to be of importance, so has immigration. Displaced Persons settled in the Upper Midwest in the late 1940s, and Soviet Jews joined them beginning in the early 1970s. Their experiences add a new dimension to the story of Jewish life in the Upper Midwest. Finally, bringing the tale up to the present day is critical in charting the developing relationship of Jewish women to their synagogues. In 1996 there were two Minnesota-born female rabbis serving Twin Cities congregations, and female cantors and synagogue presidents have become commonplace in both Reform and Conservative congregations.

"And Prairie Dogs Weren't Kosher" enlarges the picture of the Jewish-American experience both for non-Jews and for Jews themselves, many of whom are not aware of the distinctive factors contributing to the unique part of their history that unfolded in the nation's heartland. In addition, the book offers new information: Through intensive investigation of the 1910 United States manuscript census, the occupational patterns of Jewish immigrant mothers and daughters in several Twin Cities neighborhoods have been tabulated. The chapter on work contrasts this information with labor participation of Jewish women in other parts of the country as well as with that of other European immigrants to the Upper Midwest. Finally, the memories and tales gathered here comprise an illuminating complement to existing literature on the Swedish, Norwegian, German, and other ethnic groups who put down roots in the region.

The voices included in this book are drawn from a wealth of previously untapped oral accounts, family histories, and organizational records. The photographs are from regional and national public and private collections and libraries. The voices and images combine to build a story different from those presented in books that take the East Coast urban experience as the sole one in which Jewish-American life was forged. The voices are framed by essays that, successively, sketch the culture of the Old Country, the process of arrival and settling in, and the four main realms of women's lives. Taken together, these essays and voices show us how the Upper Midwestern environment molded the American experiences of several generations of Jewish women. Women shaped the Jewish lives of their families, and they shaped their Jewish communities. As wives and daughters of fur traders, homesteaders, and small-town businessmen, they are part of American history, but they must be acknowledged as ethnic women, too.

When Laura Rapaport Borsten, who was born in North Dakota in 1912 and moved to Minneapolis as a young woman, asked her mother how to make challah (Sabbath bread), she got a list of ingredients. But how much? "Until it's right," her mother replied. A history of Jewish mothers provides the basic ingredients, and the secular culture provides additional variations. But in what proportions, and how long to bake, is a woman's own choice—now more so than ever before. Jewish women have been altering the recipes for their culture since the moment they began landing in America. Even when there are new ingredients, however, the taste and the aroma remind us of our ties with the past.

CHAPTER ONE

"Like Birds Flying from Their Nest"

Life in the Old Country

April 2nd 1905. A beautiful balmy sunshine morning with buds on the trees and flowers opening to welcome the spring morning sunshine. As we were all standing on the railroad platform surrounded by all of our relatives and friends, some were talking, some were thinking, and some were crying. Especially our mother when she cried out loud and said to us, "My little flock of birds. I have sheltered you all these years under my wings and now in a few minutes you will all fly away from me and perhaps I will never see you again.". . . Everybody broke down and cried.

THUS CHARLES LOSK recalled his mother's lament at the departure from Odessa of her sons, a daughter, and their families, bound for Anamoose, North Dakota, to homestead. In the informal life history he wrote more than forty years after leaving Russia, he is silent about why his mother stayed behind.

Poignant and painful leave-takings such as this one were commonplace between the early 1880s and the mid-1920s, when more than one and one-half million Russian Jews as well as one-half million Jews from Rumania, Hungary, and Galicia emigrated to America. Statistics documenting how many Jews chose to settle in Minnesota and the Dakotas during these years are skimpy and generally unreliable, but the number was most likely somewhere above twenty thousand. Though they felt compelled to depart their homelands and were filled with hope by the seeming promise of the New World, the emigrants typically left behind family members whom, they justifiably feared, they might never see again.

The Eastern European Jews joined roughly a quarter-million Jews who were already in America, many of whom had left German-speaking countries between 1820 and 1880. This large-scale, long-lasting migration had multiple causes. Economic dislocation, rising birthrates, dashed hopes for emancipation, and outright fear for physical survival were some of the factors that, to greater or lesser degrees, led Jews to leave their native lands.

The cultural and social backgrounds of European Jews were just as varied as their reasons for leaving. For example, Jews arriving from Germanic lands came from villages and small towns where men had been cattle dealers, artisans, and minor tradesmen and

Pale of Settlement
1835 – 1917

St. Petersburg (Leningrad)

Lake Pskov

Lake Ilmen

Baltic Sea

Baltic Provinces

LITHUANIA

GERMANY

Vilna

Minsk

Moscow

RUSSIA

Warsaw

POLAND

Cracow

Lublin

Chernigov

Zhitomir

Kiev

AUSTRIA–HUNGARY

RUMANIA

UKRAINE

Kishinev

Odessa

Sea of Azov

Sebastopol

Yalta

Black Sea

0   100   200 m

0   100   200 km

where women worked in family businesses, maintained kosher homes, and raised God-fearing children. Jewish life in this milieu was traditional for men as well; they learned the rudiments of religious texts, prayed at synagogue, and cared for the welfare of the total Jewish community. Two major factors accounted for the emigration of Jews from German-speaking lands: Their traditional occupations became superfluous with changes in the agricultural economy; and their status as citizens, gained during the Napoleonic era, was rescinded during the thirty-year period of reaction that followed the Congress of Vienna in 1815. Many of the old laws and special taxes that had crimped their freedom of marriage, residence, and employment were reinstituted. Emigration provided a solution, and many younger sons were packed off to America to secure a beachhead and then send for siblings and parents.

The majority of German-speaking Jews stayed put in their countries of birth, although when they were allowed freedom to choose their place of residence, they moved to larger cities. Despite having to deal with a lack of full civil rights and endemic anti-Semitism, they managed to forge new economic, commercial, and professional roles. At the same time, a group of university-trained rabbis called for changes in religious practices. They viewed Judaism as an evolving religion and, therefore, worked to revise and, in some cases, discard many longstanding Jewish laws and customs. By the 1840s the Reform movement, as it came to be called, had a strong following in major German cities.

Jewish life in Eastern Europe held to tradition much longer than in German-speaking lands. For example, Eastern European Jews continued using Yiddish as their everyday language long after Germanic Jews had discarded it for the tongue of the majority culture. Moreover, a different set of historical circumstances prevailed in Eastern Europe. For instance, Jews had lived in Poland since the Middle Ages, when they were invited there by the ruling princes. They served as traders, artisans, and intermediaries between peasant and lord. They also built a rich communal and religious life that reached its peak in the 1600s. But as the Polish state disintegrated in the eighteenth century and was divided among Prussia, Austria-Hungary, and Russia, Jewish life became more precarious.

When Russia swallowed large chunks of Poland, one population was found to be indigestible—the Jews. Acceding to the wishes of Russian merchants to confine these new rivals, Czarina Catherine II decreed in 1772 that her new Jewish subjects had to live and trade within an area that Russia had annexed from both Poland and Turkey. The westernmost band of the country, which stretched from the Baltic to the Black Sea, became known as the Pale of Settlement. Within the Pale, Jews lived in villages and shtetls (small towns with a predominantly Jewish population) and in certain large cities such as Vilna and Odessa. They were not allowed to own land. The majority inhabited shtetls, where they continued in their traditional occupations and religious life and ran their communal affairs through a council called the kahal.

Shtetl life was characterized by rigid gender and caste divisions based both on wealth and learning. Only men were commanded to pray three times a day. They were expected and encouraged to study the sacred texts, first in the *kheyder* (religious elementary schools) and then in institutes of higher Jewish learning called yeshivas. Promising scholars were often supported for several years after marriage by their in-laws and, later, by their wives. Even ordinary tradesmen tried to set aside weekly time to study simpler texts with their *khevre* (group).* These were the ideals. The reality was that the majority of Jewish lads could not afford to finish *kheyder,* much less attend a yeshiva. Tevye, the milkman in Shalom Aleichem's stories (and the musical *Fiddler on the Roof*), is closer to the norm. He knows how to pray but cannot engage in learned discourse. He longs for time to study, but constant labor is his earthly lot.

In a culture that valued religious study over working for a living, women were prohibited from doing the former and were free, in fact encouraged, to pursue the latter. For example, a girl's education was markedly inferior to that of her brother. She started school later than her brother, at age seven or eight, and attended fewer hours per day, learning just enough Hebrew to read her prayers,

---

*A *khevre* is a group of men or women whose members pursue philanthropic, social service, or—in the case of men—educational goals.

Eastern European Jewish girls often received their religious education from female teachers.

enough Yiddish to read devotional literature and write letters, and possibly enough Russian and arithmetic to succeed in commerce. After two or three years her schooling was done. There was no perceived reason to educate her further, for it was deemed inappropriate for women to study sacred texts.

Thus equipped, she was ready to enter the work force. Daughters of the well-to-do learned the rudiments of their families' businesses, while the poorest families might send their daughters into domestic service. Almost all girls learned needlework, however. Those from better-off families did fancywork to decorate their own clothing. Girls between the ages of ten and fourteen from families that were less well-off were apprenticed to seamstresses. They might become skilled enough dressmakers to attract a wealthy clientele, or sew skirts and shirtwaists for families of modest means. Less talented needleworkers sewed for peasant women or became

Wives frequently added to the family wage by selling goods and produce in the marketplace.

itinerant seamstresses, making all the clothing, sheets, underwear, and bedclothes for a household's yearly needs.

After marriage a woman was expected, even encouraged, to combine family duties with earning a living. Needlework continued, and women also commonly sold food and produce in the market-place, owned small dry goods stores, and sometimes managed sizable family businesses. In addition, they were the shtetl's match-makers, midwives, herbalists, and bathhouse attendants.

Although Jewish women were not enjoined to attend synagogue to pray daily at set times, as were men, they prayed at home dur-ing the week and occasionally at synagogues on the Sabbath. Those who attended synagogues were segregated, either in a balcony or a special room. From there, the *zogerke* (most learned woman) acted as a prayer leader and kept the less lettered women informed about details of the service. The *zogerke* also prompted women congregants to show the proper emotion, for example, crying dur-ing the sadder prayers.

Women had a prayer book, written in Yiddish and Hebrew, called *Tsena-U'rena* (Go Forth and See). Also known as "the women's Bible," it supplied interpretations alongside prayers. A special genre of prayers called *tkhines* (from the Hebrew, meaning supplications), some of which were written by women and which related to daily life, were recited informally at home.

This culture had no place for single women. A woman's basic requirement was to become a wife and mother. Marriage was seen as a religious obligation as well as an economic union. In the shtetl, marrying for love was considered frivolous, and parents employed a shadchan (matchmaker) to broker suitable matches. Wealth, learning, *yikhes* (family status), and the relative ages of the bride and groom all played a part. There was a vast difference between being poor and being *prost*, which signified a lack of learning. A *prost* but wealthy man might arrange a marriage between his daughter and a poor but learned scholar and thereby gain prestige. The often complex negotiations culminated in the signing, just before the wedding, of a ketubah (a contract that spelled out the husband's obligations to the wife). Under Jewish law, the dowry

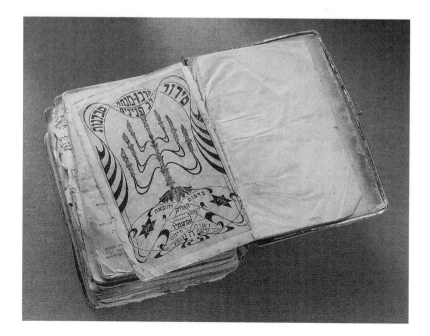

This siddur (daily prayer book) was printed in Warsaw in 1878 and brought to Minnesota. Its owner used it all her life.

was the wife's own property and had to be restored to her in case the marriage failed.

The wedding ceremony and feast were the last step. Before marriage a traditional Jewish woman had nearly all her hair cut and put on a sheitel (wig). Afterward, only her husband would see her head uncovered. Prior to the wedding she also immersed herself in the mikvah (ritual bath).

Married women had three major religious obligations: to bathe in the mikvah after each menstrual period, to separate a small portion of the challah (Sabbath bread) as a remembrance of the priestly offerings in the ancient Temple in Jerusalem, and to usher in each holy day by lighting candles.

Beyond these three imperatives, women's main religious role revolved around enforcing the dietary laws that mandated the separation of meat and milk foods and all utensils that came in contact with food. Women's direct role in the Sabbath involved lighting the candles, baking the challah, and serving a meal that included special foods. The challah, a braided white bread unlike the heavy bread eaten during the rest of the week, stood for Sabbath's separateness from the other days. The rest of the meal confirmed this distinction; depending on how much money a family had, it might consist of chicken soup, gefilte fish, roasted meat or chicken with side dishes, and a fruit compote. Mothers imparted an informal domestic religious education to their daughters as they helped in the kitchen. These were heavy responsibilities, and a wife's reward came every Sabbath eve when she was praised, in the words of the Book of Proverbs, as "a woman of valor."

Women were charged with creating the proper environment for other observances as well. Passover, the spring holiday celebrating the liberation of the Hebrews from slavery in Egypt, ironically brought with it an enormous amount of extra work. Just as the prohibition against mixing meat and milk foods entailed keeping duplicate items for almost everything used in the kitchen, so did the Passover prohibition against eating leavened food bring about its own laws and customs. (The Children of Israel had to leave Egypt so hurriedly that there was no time for their bread dough to rise.

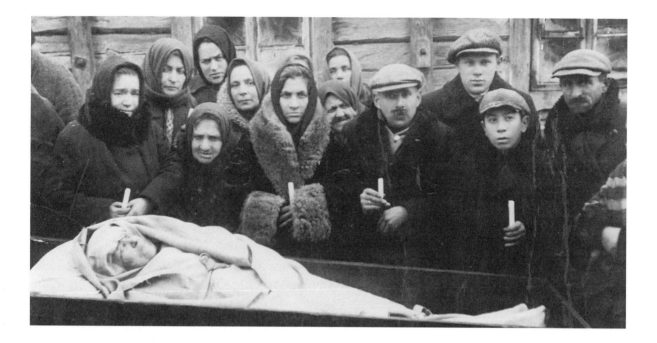

A Jewish woman's funeral in Lithuania, 1935

The unleavened cakes they were able to bake were called matzohs. In commemoration, Jews are enjoined during Passover from eating foods that contain yeast or, for example, baking powder.) A special housecleaning, a complete second set of kitchen utensils and dishes, and foods specially prepared for Passover were required. It was an expensive holiday, so expensive that a special fund, administered by the rabbi or Jewish council, existed to help those who could not afford it.

Obligations to the community fell within the purview of women as well. The women's *khevre kadishah* (burial society), a corollary to that for the men, prepared women's bodies for burial. Other women's *khevres* visited the sick, collected dowries for orphaned brides, and made sure that indigent yeshiva students were provided with clothing, meals, and books. Women also performed individual acts of tzedakah (righteousness), such as ensuring that the poor had a Sabbath meal.

·

Recent popular entertainments such as *Fiddler on the Roof* have both romanticized shtetl life and coated it with a veneer of timelessness. In truth, the shtetl was not a wholly admirable place: The wealthy and the learned controlled the kahal, the *khevre kadishah,* and other benevolent societies, and they had the best seats in the synagogues. Despite such inequalities, all shtetl inhabitants shared a religion that placed great emphasis on caring for Jews in need, and all were faced with intense anti-Semitism.

Their relations with Christians were complex. Mistrust of Russians was the norm. Those who had suffered through pogroms—orgies of vandalism and slaughter—were downright fearful. Nevertheless, some Jews survived persecution because Russian neighbors protected them. Jews who belonged to the intelligentsia or to banned political groups often had worked alongside ethnic Russians to overthrow the czar. Other Jews had carried on trade relations with German-Russian farmers in the Ukraine, who were not prone to violence. In general, however, bitter experience had taught Eastern European Jews to expect help from each other rather than from Christians.

That help was not always forthcoming—an indication that cracks, both economic and political, were appearing in the veneer of Jewish society. They were the result of potent new ideas. Hasidism, a movement that addressed the spiritual yearnings of common people and was characterized by ecstatic prayer and charismatic leadership, and the Haskalah, the Jewish counterpart of the Enlightenment, had created deep divisions within Russian-Jewish communities during the eighteenth century. Newer political movements rooted in the Haskalah developed in the later nineteenth century, further disrupting the old caste patterns. One such movement was Zionism, which proclaimed that nationalism was the only solution to Jewish rootlessness and European anti-Semitism. The movement began in Russia as a reaction to the first pogroms in 1881 and 1882 and gained greater popularity when Theodor Herzl, an Austrian Jew and journalist, began actively advocating the establishment of a Jewish state. This stance was antithetical to many rabbis, who felt that only God could reclaim the ancient homeland. Although it was illegal, the Zionist movement continued to grow until, by 1917, it had some three hundred thousand members in the Russian empire.

Another illegal movement was the Bund, the socialist organization founded in 1897 that worked to unify Jewish workers and directed efforts to overthrow the czar, establish a socialist democracy in Russia, and retain a large measure of cultural autonomy for Jews. Offering revolutionary promises of a better future, Bundism pitted the new Jewish proletariat against Jewish factory owners as well as against rabbis. Given this atmosphere of turmoil and stress, it is not surprising that, by 1890, some men's *khevres* turned into proto-trade unions.

In textile and knitting mills and in cigarette and cigar factories, some young working women also became ardent Bundists. Leaders of the Bund often taught these women to read Russian, discussed economics with them, and explained to them the roots of workers' own exploitation. For many young women, this was the first time their educational aspirations were taken seriously. They then carried the struggle to the factories and shops, persuading others to join the Bund. Despite becoming socialists, however, many women maintained sentimental attachments to their religion—or at least to its customs. Women could be kosher Bundists, Sabbath-candle-lighting socialists.

There were a number of reasons for the growth of Zionism and the Bund. During the late nineteenth and early twentieth centuries, the Jewish community of the Pale as a whole was becoming both larger and poorer, due to various economic, political, demographic, and social changes. Changes in agricultural practices had also disrupted the lives of Jews in the countryside and pushed increasing numbers of them into the cities. Industrialization was making the work that artisans once performed outmoded: They were forced to labor in factories for lower wages. Women and children had the lowest-paid jobs in the cigarette, knitting, and textile industries.

Jews also were growing poorer because of a high birthrate and

Victims of a pogrom in the
Ukraine, about 1919

a relatively low death rate. In Russia and Poland the Jewish population rose from approximately one and one-half million in 1820
to five and one-half million in 1910. Additionally, they were getting
poorer because the laws governing where they could live and what
occupations they could pursue were becoming ever more restric-
tive. The most onerous of these were the so-called May Laws. Instituted following the March 1881 assassination of the liberal Czar
Alexander II, these laws marked a turning point in Russia's treatment of its Jews. Although a nihilist had killed his father, Alexander
III made Jews the scapegoats. The May Laws expelled Jews from
villages where they had long lived, barred them from doing business on Sundays and Christian holidays (they were already con-
strained from working on the Sabbath and other Jewish holidays),
forbade them from pursuing certain livelihoods such as owning
taverns, and subjected them to severe school-admission quotas.

Finally, the Russian government allowed pogroms to take place,
particularly in the Ukraine and White Russia. The largest of these
occurred in 1881, 1882, 1903, and 1905, but the threat was constant. While it is not clear whether the government actually ordered

the pogroms, it unmistakably encouraged peasants to believe that Jews were the cause of their poverty, then did nothing to prevent brutal attacks. The government's overall attitude toward its Jewish subjects was epitomized not only by the May Laws but also by the goals attributed to Konstantin Pobedonostsev, an influential adviser to czars Alexander III and Nicholas II. He projected that one-third of Russia's Jews would be killed, one-third would be made to leave the country, and one-third would be converted to Christianity. The first part of his projection was becoming a reality as pogroms continued and hunger spread. One measure of this was the number of applicants for Passover charity, which by the turn of the century rose to almost 20 percent of the Pale's Jewish population. Since the majority of Jews would not consider conversion, the solution was to emigrate. And emigrate many of them did.

A high birthrate and relatively low death rate, an industrialization that pauperized artisans, a factory system whose hiring practices favored Christians, laws restricting where Jews could live and what sorts of jobs they could hold, the ever-present threat of pogroms, the loss of hope for a more democratic government after the failed revolution of 1905, and the stagnating shtetl economy—all these factors pushed Jews out of Russia. Letters from relatives and countrymen who had established themselves in America and who provided steamship tickets supplied the pull. Jewish organizations assisted Eastern European Jews embarking from major ports such as Bremen, Hamburg, and Liverpool with advice, refreshments, and temporary shelter.

Women made up almost half of this migration. Unlike Swedish or Irish women, for example, Jewish women migrated either in family units or in order to join kin already in America—a process known as "chain migration." In this process, family members, generally young males most likely to find employment, were the first to emigrate. Once employed in America, they scrimped and saved to finance the subsequent emigration of younger brothers and sisters. All then pooled resources to bring over the less economically productive elders. Like the Irish but unlike Italians or members of many Slavic groups, Jews arrived in the United States intending to stay.

Between 1880 and 1920, the rate of Jews returning to Europe was well below 10 percent, while the overall total among immigrants was about 33 percent.

Mothers arrived carrying *peckelakh* (bundles), which contained their most valuable possessions, such as candlesticks, favorite spoons, prayer books, embroidered challah and matzoh covers, feather pillows and *perenes* (feather quilts), samovars, books, and photographs of parents left behind. They carried dried bread in wicker baskets, enough to feed the family in case kosher food was not available. In a real sense, the *peckelakh* contained their material culture.

What was not carried in the bundles was part of the mindset—the duties of a Jewish wife to maintain a kosher home and raise children who would become *mentschen* (responsible adults); the necessity of working alongside or instead of husbands or fathers to

Peckelakh (bundles) included ritual objects such as candlesticks, kiddush cups, prayer books, and matzoh covers; practical items such as samovars, towels embroidered with Russian proverbs, pots, and rolling pins; wedding documents; and photographs of relatives left behind in the Old Country.

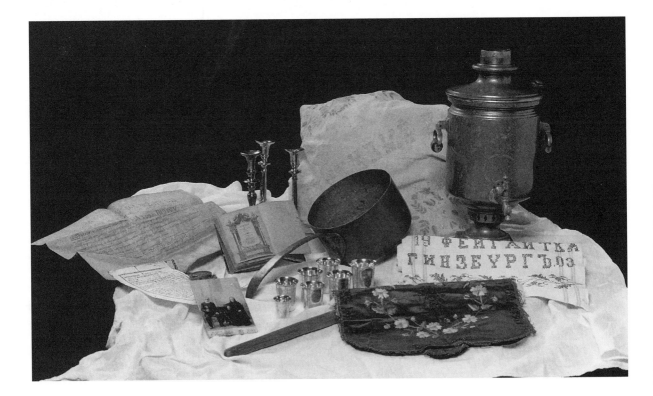

earn *parnoseh* (a living); the need to bathe in the mikvah and attend synagogue; and the obligation to provide tzedakah.

Such was the basic context of life for European Jewish women from the mid-1800s to the opening decades of the 1900s. The oral and written record personalizes that context. In specific and often vivid terms, the women—and here, some men—who immigrated depict the existence they left behind and the frequently brutal circumstances that drove them to embark on an uncertain future in a distant land.

VOICES

HIGH PRIESTESS AND DRUDGE

A woman's domestic role could exalt her or keep her close to the earth. It all depended on one's attitude. The following selection is from an unpublished novel, "Call Me Marah," by Sarah Cohen Berman of Minneapolis. She began writing it after visiting the Soviet Union in 1933 and finished probably during World War II. Berman portrays Jewish family life before and after the Russian Revolution of 1917, perhaps drawing on her own experiences.

The household tasks which for the Jewish housewife are sanctified, because they have acquired a religious significance, became mere drudgery without it. The preparations for the Sabbath and the festivals, even the housecleaning for Passover, were performed in a spirit of religious exaltation. The hard-working housewife was a priestess performing the commands of God. She was not a mere drudge. The Sabbaths and festivals broke the monotony of life and brought gaiety and joy to the most dreary of lives.

———

The Katz family lived in Berdichev, a town in the Ukraine. Because her family was quite poor, Sophie, the eldest child, went to work at age nine, in about 1897. Of course, she also helped her mother at home.

Thursday, I used to help her baking bread and fixing the house. And I used to remind myself, tomorrow is Friday.

Tomorrow is Friday night. My father comes home, he goes to the bath, puts on a clean shirt and fixes himself up, puts on the holiday clothes. Mother is bathed and washed . . . she wore a little scarf to protect her hair, because she's supposed to wear a wig. . . . And I used to come home Friday a little earlier from work, and it was so peaceful. The challah, the beautiful bread that she finished baking, and it was so clean and every child was washed and dressed, and it was so beautiful it gave me the greatest thrill in the world. I used to come fast home. . . . [Mother] had a little money, but she used it up for the Sabbath. . . . Monday there is no bread, she has to start baking, and the same little house becomes like a panic. . . . And I used to many times feel so low down, but I went to work and it went on, the week. And usually the week was for worries.

WORK

Solomon Bailin, whose family emigrated in 1911 from Sosnitza, a Ukrainian village near Chernigov, to Sioux City, Iowa, recalled his mother as the economic mainstay of the family and the driving force in their emigration. His description of their life in Russia is interlaced with bits of unmistakably American terminology.

We were very poor. . . . My mother had two cows, and from the two cows she managed to feed seven of us. The butter, cheese, and milk she sold . . . paid for our schooling in the little village. . . . My father was a cattle buyer and had no money. . . . [He] finally struck a piece of luck. He and his two partners happened to go to a great big ranch and bought a big lot of cattle. They sent the cattle to St. Petersburg market and happened to strike a good market.* They made $39,000 on that big lot of cat-

---

*St. Petersburg was outside the Pale of Settlement, but one could obtain a temporary-residence permit in order to buy and sell there, as Bailin's father must have done.

tle. Naturally, my father was overjoyed. He came home, and in an old suitcase he had $13,000 in cash. . . . My mother was over-joyed. The first thing she did was pay her debts . . . [and she] bought some clothes for the family, and we were all happy. My father stayed at home for about a week or ten days. Then he thought he was very smart and decided to go back and try his luck again with his partners. He took $3000 with him in cash, and about three weeks later he came home without a penny in his pocket. . . . My mother was a very clever woman and knew what she was doing. She told him, "Nothing doing. [You had one good strike.] You are not getting [the remaining] money. We have been poor long enough. With this money here we are going to America."

Young Sophie Katz was apprenticed first to a hatmaker and then to several dressmakers. As she remembered, "You got no money to apprentice for three, four years, but you used to work twelve hours a day, sometimes fourteen." Her father had been injured in an industrial accident, and so her family needed money immediately. A friend employed at a bentwood chair factory helped her obtain a job putting in screws, sanding down rough spots, and varnishing.

After a month's work, my friend called in the manager of the factory and says, "Look, this little girl is quite young, but, boy, look at her work." . . . And she talked him into giving me a trial of two dozen chairs. She said, "If her work isn't good, I will guar-antee it and make it up to you." So he agreed.

I've always had very thin skin, so for weeks my hands were swollen from the varnish. I used to come home and soak them. I was afraid to tell my mother how much I suffered from that, because she would stop me from working; even though we need-ed money, they would rather starve than have me suffer. . . . Little by little my hands got stronger. You see, I didn't varnish the chairs with a brush but with a cheese cloth. I used to go around and around the chair, and after six months, I made a bend in the floor. There was a bend in me, too.

Well, the manager gave me the two dozen chairs, and I finished them before the time I was supposed to. He was very pleased and said I could keep on. My first wages from those chairs was just six or seven rubles, and he gave me all silver rubles. I'll tell you, until I got down the hill where we lived, I was making double-long steps. I came in with that money and said, "Mom, we're rich now; look what I made." . . . I used to bring home every penny to give to my mother.

PRAYER, GOOD DEEDS, AND SOCIAL ACTION

Edith Modelevsky's family lived in Pulan, a village near Zhitomir in southwestern Russia, from 1901 to 1912. Her mother recited this tkhine *after the havdalah ceremony, which marks the end of the Sabbath.*

Then it was time for Mama to give the prayer of women . . . for protection of the family during the week to come. . . .

> *God of Abraham, Isaac and Jacob,*
> *The Holy Sabbath passes away;*
> *May the new week come to us*
> *For health, life and all good;*
> *May it bring us sustenance, good things,*
> *Deliverance and consolations. Amen.*

It was said in Yiddish, just as her greeting to the Sabbath. It is an important prayer, for it is filled with concern for the daily problems of making a living.

———

Sophie Turnoy Trupin enlarged the picture of women's devotional life in describing her devout grandmother, who remained behind in Seltz, a Polish-Russian shtetl, when Sophie, her mother, a sister, and two brothers emigrated in 1908 to join her father. He had left in 1904, after a pogrom, and was homesteading near Wilton, North Dakota.

My grandmother was small, fragile, and very devout. She wore a black silk dress and a *sheitel*, or wig, of straight black hair over which she wore a black wool shawl. She was a widow and made her living by running a little dry goods store. She arose before dawn every day of the week, put up the samovar with charcoal and water, and went out to purchase fresh bagels and *halvah*, which she left on the dining room table. Before opening her store, she went to *shul* to pray. . . . Also, once a week she prepared a basket of food for some poor family who otherwise would have little with which to usher in the Sabbath. Her life was devoted to work, prayer, and charity.

———

The Bund appealed to working girls such as Sophie Katz because it offered them educational opportunities and, within its organizational structure, chances to perform the same tasks as men.

Through this group I became quite a little organizer. Some of the leaders gave me a job to organize the shop girls. . . . I was very aggressive; I could do a lot of things other girls wouldn't try. But they started telling me, "You're too young, you need more education. If you're not careful, the police will throw you in jail."

Sophie found a teacher in the Bund.

She gave me things to read. In classes they would sit and read and explain to us how things developed over time, how capitalism developed. . . . [E]verything we did . . . had to be underground, secret . . . because the stronger the revolutionaries got . . . the stronger the police tried to watch them.

THE PULL FACTORS

Correspondence from America was an enormously influential factor in persuading family members to chance the arduous journey. Sarah Thal, who arrived in Wisconsin in the early 1880s, is one of the few German-Jewish women who recorded her experiences in the Upper Midwest. She described what appears to have been a solely economic decision to emigrate.

I grew to womanhood in the town of Ellingen in the Saar Valley, and when I married Solomon Thal, in 1880, I went to live in the picturesque village of Berg in the Mosel Valley. I remember this country as quiet and picturesque, where life was pleasant and peaceful.

My husband had brothers in Milwaukee who sent home glowing reports of conditions in America. We wished to try our luck in that wonderful land. When my daughter, Elsie, was fourteen months old we left to make our fortune fully confident of our undertaking.

––––––

Poor Jewish women had few marriage choices in the tradition-choked culture of the shtetl. America offered a way out to those who sought it.

Sarah Cohen Berman's unpublished novel, "Call Me Marah" (about 1933–1945), depicts the family of a rabbi with seven daughters. Although poor, their yikhes *prevents most of them from working for a living. Fögele, Marah's older sister, defies convention by soliciting work and then further scandalizes the family by eloping to America.*

All of us were accomplished needlewomen, so Fögele braved public opinion and went out among the well-to-do families, offering to do fancy sewing and embroidery. In the course of time she procured enough work to keep us all busy. At first she was scolded for lowering our dignity, but the money thus earned was so wel-

Many Jewish women in the Russian empire worked in small tailor shops and knitting factories or as dressmakers.

come that eventually we acquiesced, and worked late into the night to prepare trousseaus for girls economically more fortunate than ourselves.

One day Fögele was gone, leaving a note entreating forgiveness. She had married Mendel Stolarov, a young carpenter, and with him left for America. She [wrote that she] was "tired of waiting for foolish pedigrees, and for pale emaciated good for nothing young men. Mendel had loved her secretly for years, and rabbi's daughter or no—it makes no difference in America where all are free and equal. There work with the hands is no disgrace."

———

Born in 1876, Rachel Bella Kahn worked as a domestic for better-off members of her extended family in Belaya Tserkov in the Ukraine. There, she met and fell in love with a butcher's assistant. She was told in no uncertain terms that such a marriage could never take place, as it would lower the yikhes *of her family.*

It appears that although I was no joy to my relatives, I was capable of bringing them disgrace. A butcher was considered hardly better than a convict, and especially so to my grandfather. . . . I reached my eighteenth birthday and my prospects for the future were now very poor. Most girls of eighteen were married in those days, and here I was a servant girl in my aunt's home without resources. I was ashamed of my status as a menial. I had no dowry to enable me to marry anyone of status. My future seemed hopeless.

Rachel escaped spinsterhood by agreeing to marry a man in North Dakota, Abraham Calof, whom her great uncle recommended and who had sent passage money upon receiving a report of her qualifications.

Finally the exchange of pictures was made. I liked his looks and he wrote that he was pleased with my appearance as well. I then corresponded with him, and although he eventually became my husband, the way was neither quick nor easy.

THE PUSH FACTORS

A particularly terrible pogrom took place in Odessa in 1905. At least three hundred Jews were killed and thousands wounded. Tens of thousands were ruined economically. Yet in Odessa, non-Jewish university students and sailors rallied to help the Jews—in part because, as groups seeking reform, they also feared attack. In shtetls and small towns, Jews generally had no gentiles to whom to turn. The following account from Odessa is by a young pharmacist, Noah Schlasinger, who was rooming with the family of his fiancée, Sarah Bendersky.

In October 1905 there was talk in Odessa that the police were going to start a pogrom. The Jewish settlements all over the city got warnings, by the grapevine, to form organizations in their neighborhoods to protect themselves. And it wasn't only Jews who were going to be attacked. Gentiles were scared too. Gentiles helped the Jews. Men came from the Black Sea docks—mutineers from the cruiser [*Potemkin*]—they came to help.

About ten of us—young men—organized our building and took turns watching. I was living with the Benderskys, in a two-story apartment house with a big heavy iron gate in front, and we kept that locked. I remember we had fog every night and it was hard to see when we were on watch.

The pogrom started in the night, away from our section of town, down near the seashore. They were burning warehouses, and we could see the flames. We were scared all right! We didn't have anything to defend ourselves with—just knives we collected, and rocks. And we moved all the women and children to the second floor of the building, and kept boiling water on the stoves to pour down in case we were attacked. And I took home a small amount of sulphuric acid from the drug store to use if we had to.

One night, when we were on watch, a *droshky* (cab) driver stopped and came over to us and asked, "Do you have anything [with which] to defend yourselves?" When we told him "No," he gave us three weapons—a Finnish hunting knife, a whip made of a door spring and a lead weight, and a revolver with some ammunition. None of us had ever had a gun—it wasn't permitted for Jews in Russia—and if you had one you could get killed by the police. Well, I put that gun in my pocket. The cab driver told us the students at the University of Odessa had been hiding away weapons for a long time, and now they were distributing them to Jewish settlements all over the city.

All through that night we heard disturbances but the pogrom didn't come into our district. I decided to go into the house to try to calm down Sarah and her family—they were inside, terribly scared, and the women were crying. Well, I did that, and as it turned out, we had a very close call. I was in the house just a few minutes, and when I came back to the gate the other men told me the police had come past the house checking to see what's going on. Our men got a warning, from a stranger who called from across the street, and they managed to slip back quietly into the yard, so the police didn't see them. If they had been seen, the police would have questioned them and there would have been trouble. And if I had been out there, with a gun in my pocket, they would have taken me away, and the others too. And we would never have come out alive.

———

From 1918 to 1921, in the wake of the Russian Revolution, the Ukraine was a battleground where White Russians, anarchists, nationalists, bandits, and Communists fought for control. Except for the latter, all acted with extreme cruelty toward the Jews, and almost 10 percent of Ukrainian Jews lost their lives. Semon Petliura, leader of the Ukrainian nationalist army, either could not or would not restrain his troops from brutally assaulting Jews in every village and town they captured. These actions drove Jews into the Communist movement, which they saw as their only salvation.

In 1923 Edith Modelevsky, fourteen years old and a recent arrival in St. Paul, wrote down for a school assignment the terrors she and her family had witnessed.

We left Russia because every month or week some other bandits came and . . . began to kill the people from the town. In 1919 Petliura came to Zhitomir and he began to kill the [Jews]. . . . [It] was about three o'clock that five soldiers came in our house and said to my mother that she should give them . . . all the money we have. . . . They took the hundred dollars [that their father had sent for passage] and threw them in my mother's face and told her that . . . isn't enough for them. My grandmother was with us so she told them that we haven't got any more money to give them so they can do with us what they please. After my grandmother said that so they told us to stand near the wall and they are going to kill us. When I heard that I was trying to run out and call somebody for help. While I was [running] to the door one bandit pushed me so hard that I fell. . . . [Then] they took the guns to shoot us so one soldier said something to the rest of them and they did not shoot us. They took away the hundred dollars and took away all our clothes and they broke our furniture and then went away.

PACKING UP

Women were responsible for packing the bundles that they or their children carried. The importance placed on keeping kosher is clear in each of the following memories.

Rose Berman Goldstein recounted how her maternal grandmother, Libby Cohen, and her five children left Lithuania around

A home vandalized in the infamously brutal 1903 pogrom in Kishinev, about one hundred miles from Odessa

Members of the Nilva and Taran
families just before they left
Russia in 1912. Their passport
stamp is at right.

ТАЛОНЪ.

Выданъ _Киевск_ _Губернатор_

_1912 г._ _Апрѣлъ 24_ дня, за № _2478ельница_

Ниму Лейби Ицковичу Нильвь съ

женою Сурой, дочерью Басей и сыномъ

Шлемомъ Отмѣтка штемпелемъ.

О выѣздѣ за границу.	О возвращеніи изъ-за границы.

Сей талонъ отрѣзывается въ пограничной Таможнѣ, въ доказательство
явки паспорта.

1890, traveling via the port of Hamburg. Her husband awaited the family in Minneapolis.

The Cohens left Kalwaria in the spring of 1892 in a horse-drawn covered wagon, . . . and reached the German border in a day or so. . . . Their baggage was in a tarpaulin roll: linens, feather-beds, copper pots, a mortar and pestle, Sabbath candlesticks, and Bobe Libby's favorite wooden rollingpin. They carried a wicker hamper of food, mostly dried pumpernickel. . . . The ship supplied potatoes, herring, vegetables, and hot biscuits, but they refused the ship's food, because it wasn't kosher.

———

Morris Tenenbaum's mother and four siblings left Lithuania in 1905 to join family members in St. Paul.

Suitcases and wardrobe trunks were not in fashion or available in the village, and, they cost money. The packing was done in large bundles. Everything to be shipped was placed on heavy sheets and down-feather comforters and tied with ropes made by a local rope maker. . . . The bundling of our possessions was so expertly done that everything arrived in the u.s.a. in perfect condition, including the glassware, china, copperware and sealed bottles of Vodka for Father, as well as the musty ocean odor that penetrated everything for a long time. . . . [W]e lunched on food we always carried with us in wicker baskets. Two kinds of dried bread, one plain and one topped with sugar. For real flavor we had jars of shmaltz (cooked chicken fat).

———

In 1908 Sophie Turnoy traveled with her mother and brothers from Seltz, in Russian Poland, to North Dakota.

The [ship's] galley and dining room were on a raised platform; at one end there was a huge table with benches around it. I don't remember any of the adults ever partaking of the food served here; perhaps it was because it was not considered kosher. Their

A Russian-Jewish woman about to emigrate says a final goodbye to her daughter, early 1970s.

main fare consisted of *suchares*, or dehydrated bread, which each family had prepared before departure. Such bread withstood mold and could sustain life.

DEPARTING

Leaving relatives behind was no easy task, for Jews knew they would probably not make the return voyage and that some relatives might never be able to join them in America.

Craney Goldman Bellin related that the 1905 Odessa pogrom sparked the departure of various younger members of the Goldman and related Losk families. Her grandmother, who remained behind because an eye disease made her ineligible for admission to the United States, lamented their departure. "My children are like birds flying from their nest," *she told her family.* "And I shall probably never see them again."

————

Benjamin N. Berger set off from the Polish shtetl of Ostrowiec in 1913, traveling with an uncle and the uncle's two daughters to join family in Fargo, North Dakota.

I left Poland . . . August 10, 1913. . . . Papa cried. . . . [T]he first time in my life that I had ever seen him cry. Mama cried, too, and that brought tears to my eyes as well. Just before I got on board, Mama took my arm and stopped me. . . . She raised her hands above her, over my head, and *"benched"* me. She asked in this blessing that the good angel watch over me and take care of me for all time, wherever I went.

————

Leah Lisovsky's family had endured much hardship in Odessa during World War I and the Russian Revolution. They finally decided to join relatives in Minneapolis.

[December 1923:] The saddest day of my father's life was the day he said goodbye to his sister, who was ill, knowing full well that he would not see his sister again. . . . I remember that I could not stop crying that day. I wondered . . . was it really worth all of our efforts to separate ourselves from our family? Then I thought about my mother, who was separated from her family, and I felt that for her sake we should. . . . The letters were coming from our grandparents that we should leave as soon as we could, because the quota, allowing people to leave Russia, was being closed. . . . The day was gray and the mist rising around the station matched the tears rising in our eyes, as we turned towards our friends and started to embrace them for the last time.

———

Willy Schwarz was born in Lechenich, a small town in the Rhineland, in 1906. His family had lived there for several hundred years. In 1938 he fled to Trinidad, one of the few countries that would take Jews escaping Germany. In 1940 he was admitted into the United States. He farmed outside St. Paul and worked as a cattle buyer in the South St. Paul stockyards.

My mother was a charitable woman. She never forgot the poor people. She cooked always for ten, fifteen people. We always went to visit the old people and brought along a dinner in little containers—one on top of another. One was soup, another was potatoes. As kids we learned to be charitable. A lot of the older people, the gentiles, had nobody. My mother closed a lot of their eyes. . . . [O]n the way to Amsterdam to get away, to get to South America, I saw my mother. She stood and she said: "I'll never see you again, but you'll be all right. I give you my blessing." That was the last I saw my mother. She ended up in the gas oven.

CHAPTER TWO

"The End of the World"
Settling in the Upper Midwest

Dreams and fancies of life flitted through my brain lessening the sorrow of parting from friends and relations and sweetening the thoughts of the privations that I had been told were before me. I remembered, then, that when my husband had asked me before our marriage what dowery [sic] my father would give me, I told him: "I know not how much he has; but I do know that I shall take nothing from him as he has a large family to care for. In America, though, any one who will work and be economical can earn money for themselves. We are young, and, in order that we may not be in want in old age and that we may honestly earn a competence, I shall go with you to the end of the world."
But when we started up the river at noon on that bright May day I did not think that the time to go to "the end of the world" had come so soon.

THUS AMELIA ULLMANN recalled her state of mind and her vows as she embarked on a sternwheeler heading up the Mississippi River to St. Paul in 1855 to join her husband, Joseph, after almost a year's separation. Born in the Rhineland area of the German states around 1830, Amelia immigrated with her family to St. Louis, where she married and gave birth to her first child before journeying to St. Paul. She was one of the first Jewish women to settle in the Upper Midwest. Full of fortitude, daring, and trepidation, Ullmann and the Jewish women who followed her moved to the "end of the world" because they hoped to find a brighter economic future. Often, however, they were girded with more faith than knowledge. They settled in large and small towns alike and even staked their own homestead claims on the plains. In the long history of the Diaspora—the scattering of the Tribes of Israel—Jews have often been minority populations in their host countries. But rarely had their number been so small, or their host country so raw or so vast. In such a land these women made their new lives.

To understand these women's lives it is necessary to see what drew them to the Upper Midwest—how the regional economy grew and how the land was made available to them—as well as to know something about the people among whom they settled.

The first thing to learn, however, is how the immigrants got to the Upper Midwest. Ullmann, like many of the pioneer German Jews, arrived by river. The early history of Europeans in the Upper Midwest is primarily a story of rivers: The St. Paul that Ullmann's sternwheeler carried her to had been founded only about a decade earlier. It was sited in safe proximity to Fort Snelling, which sat on a rocky outcrop at the confluence of the Mississippi and Minnesota Rivers. From there, army officers could literally oversee the river trade of people such as Ullmann's husband. He eventually became a fur trader, buying the skins in St. Paul and shipping them to Europe.

The quest for furs was the first commercial venture undertaken by both Indians and Europeans in the region. Success in pursuing

Amelia Ullmann, one of the first Jewish women to settle in St. Paul. Oil portrait by Thomas Cantwell Healy, 1857.

this enterprise depended on the trader's ability to maintain good relations with the Indians. The largest groups of people in the Upper Midwest were the Ojibway and Dakota, who inhabited the vast area of forest and plains that became Minnesota and the Dakotas. For example, Maurice Mordecai Samuel, a Jewish fur trader active in the St. Croix River valley in the 1840s, is said to have been on excellent terms with the local Ojibway. He followed a common practice in his trade by marrying an Ojibway woman. The Missouri River provided access from St. Louis to the Dakotas, where Jews began settling in the 1860s, all the way to Fort Benton, in Montana Territory.

Furs, minerals, timber, agricultural lands, and later, in the cities, a developing manufacturing and commercial economy—all drew European emigrants into the Upper Midwest. With the white settlers' hunger for agricultural land, the Ojibway and Dakota of Minnesota were forced, between 1837 and 1889, to cede their richest lands and move onto reservations. Old-Stock Americans (people of European background whose families had resided in America for several generations), Canadians, Germans, and Scandinavians moved onto former Indian land to harvest timber and to farm. Dakota Territory was opened to settlers beginning in 1859 as the Dakota, Lakota, and Nakota, as well as the Cree, Crow, Cheyenne, Mandan, and Arikara, were compelled to give up their lands.

The most spectacular population growth occurred from the 1850s to the 1890s, largely as the result of the national railroad network reaching and then spreading throughout the region. The new ease and lower cost of transportation further opened the Upper Midwest for agriculture and mining and swelled the new cities with Scandinavians, Germans, Irish, and Canadians. A common route for immigrants was by rail from the eastern ports via Chicago to the Twin Cities. Still others traveled through Canada and via Winnipeg to the Dakotas. Towns such as Mankato and St. Cloud in Minnesota, Sioux Falls and Aberdeen in South Dakota, and Fargo and Grand Forks in North Dakota's Red River valley grew as railroad terminuses and commercial centers for the agricultural hinterlands.

The discovery of gold in the Black Hills during the mid-1870s brought hordes of treasure seekers to what later became South Dakota. Although the Black Hills were secured for the Lakota by treaty, this was no impediment to gold miners. (The Jewish section of the Mount Moriah cemetery in the town of Deadwood testifies to their participation in the gold rush.) However, agriculture, in the form of wheat cultivation, proved to be a more lasting treasure for the Dakotas. Railroad-company publicity touted the prairie to prospective settlers as fertile land, and the Homestead Act, passed in 1862, made it easy for the new arrivals to start farming. All one needed was to pay a registration fee of $10, move onto the 160-acre allotment within six months, and improve it by plowing, planting, and establishing a residence. After five years, a final "proving up" fee of $4 was required for ownership.

The easy terms of the Homestead Act brought settlers to what is now North Dakota from Norway, Germany, and Russia to join the already established population groups. The Russian group was primarily composed of Catholic and Protestant German-Russians, that is, Germans who had been invited by Russian rulers between 1770 and 1804 to farm in the regions of the lower Volga River and around the Black Sea. They left for America to seek new land and to escape growing tensions with the czarist government. In present-day South Dakota, too, Norwegians, German nationals, and German-Russians predominated. These were the people among whom the Jews settled.

In Minnesota the bedrock enterprises, in addition to farms, were sawmills, flour mills, and iron-ore mines. The southern and western portions of the state contained rich farmland, and until the early twentieth century the northern sections were covered with valuable timber. Towns such as Stillwater, Hinckley, Cloquet, and Virginia grew wealthy from their sawmills, while Minneapolis became known as the mill city due to the number of flour mills situated on the banks of the Mississippi River. The rich ore deposits of the Mesabi Iron Range in northern Minnesota began to draw a new wave of immigrants from the southern, central, and eastern parts of Europe, as well as Finns. From the 1890s to the 1920s, the Iron

Range towns and Duluth, the transshipment port for the ore, all flourished.

.

The first groups of Jews to enter the Upper Midwest had emigrated from German-speaking lands. Arriving in the 1850s and 1860s, many had already lost their immigrant "greenness" by peddling or by clerking in mercantile establishments east of the Mississippi. Economic opportunity pulled them to the Upper Midwest to trade with Indians for furs, to speculate in land, to open stores and small manufacturing concerns in the new river towns, to mine gold in the Black Hills, and, less frequently, to farm.

Amelia Ullmann's husband, Joseph, based his fur-trading business in St. Paul. At roughly the same time, Hannah Austrian's husband, Julius, traded on Madeleine Island, near Bayfield, Wisconsin. Hannah lived on the island for twelve years among Ojibway and missionary neighbors. There she reared her children, singing them Hebrew songs that she played on her banjo. In the 1880s, Sarah Thal and her family lived on a farm in what is now Nelson County, in eastern North Dakota. Her neighbors were a mix of immigrants and Old-Stock Americans.

Most German-Jewish women were not quite so isolated. In general terms, the German Jews, most of whom arrived between 1850 and 1880, settled in significant numbers in St. Paul, Minneapolis, Duluth, and, for a short time, in Deadwood. In these places they became merchants and manufacturers. Amelia Ullmann was the first Jewish woman who recorded her arrival in St. Paul, but there were certainly others in the town. In 1856, a year after she debarked, there were about twenty-five Jewish men and women—enough to form the Mount Zion Hebrew Association. Six years later it became Mount Zion Hebrew Congregation.

The Minneapolis Jewish community grew as well, and, in 1878, German Jews there founded Shaari Tof [sic] Hebrew Congregation, which was later renamed Temple Israel. By the 1880s, German-Jewish merchants could generally be found in every sizable market town or transportation center in the region. Sioux Falls and Aberdeen in

Members of the Feinstein family of Zeeland, North Dakota, about 1890

present-day South Dakota; Fargo, Grand Forks, and Bismarck in what is now North Dakota; and Mankato, Austin, Le Sueur, and Albert Lea in Minnesota—all had one or two Jewish families. Many maintained their ties to larger Jewish communities through synagogue affiliations, while others drifted away from Jewish practices. Often, family ties connected members through the region. For example, in turn-of-the-century St. Paul, the Plechner-Fantle family of furniture and clothing merchants spotted fertile business ground in the thriving divorce-mill town of Sioux Falls (the Reno, Nevada, of its day). Espying opportunity in the enforced leisure of estranged and bored spouses, they dispatched relatives there to open another store.

The second, and much larger wave of migration to America—and the Upper Midwest—began in the early 1880s and consisted of Eastern European Jews, primarily from the Russian empire and Rumania. They were helped westward, and ultimately across the ocean, by Jewish communities along the way. The process did not stop at the East Coast. One example was the band of two hundred people who arrived in St. Paul by train in July 1882 without warning. Their sudden appearance overtaxed the resources of the members of Mount Zion Congregation, who gratefully accepted help from Christian citizens of the city.

Immigration from Eastern Europe continued to grow as a response to push factors such as pogroms and to pull factors such as encouraging letters and travel money from friends and relatives who had settled in the Upper Midwest. Except for an interruption during World War I, migration did not cease until the United States, mainly by means of the Johnson-Reed Act (1924), called a virtual halt to immigration from Eastern and Southern Europe.

Many Jews were assisted by the Industrial Removal Office (IRO), an East Coast Jewish organization that attempted to settle Jews inland, away from the overcrowded ghettos and "gateway districts" of the largest eastern cities. The IRO also dealt with immigrants funneled through the port of Galveston, Texas, and then transported up the Mississippi to the Midwest. In both cases, members of the national Jewish fraternal organization, B'nai Brith (Sons of the Covenant), found them jobs throughout the region.

Like other immigrants, Jews also entered the United States via the Great Lakes, a route that enabled them to avoid the turmoil of Ellis Island and save money. Other Jews came through Canada. A ticket from Liverpool, England, to Winnipeg cost Norton Giller's family $25 in the early 1890s. The train from there to Grand Forks, one hundred miles away, cost them a penny per mile. Giller recounted that "for one dollar they came to 'America.'"

Once they had arrived, the Eastern European Jews needed work. Unlike New York City, St. Paul and Minneapolis did not have a large garment industry. Also, Jews do not appear to have worked in the burgeoning flour or lumber mills. Other forms of factory work, peddling, and small-business ownership characterized the economic life of the newer arrivals.

Immigrants who arrived in the Twin Cities generally settled in neighborhoods near the downtowns, where the rent was cheap and the houses were close to work. Housing mainly consisted of single dwellings and duplexes, for land was inexpensive and tenements, therefore, relatively rare. St. Paul had two Jewish districts, the West Side and the Capitol City area. Minneapolis had its North Side, composed of Jews from the Russian empire, and its South Side, filled with Rumanians. While these areas had large proportions of Jews, they were never confined solely to one ethnic group. The North Side of Minneapolis was shared by African Americans, Irish, and Old-Stock Americans; the West Side of St. Paul, by Poles, Syrians, and Mexicans.

Smaller cities as well had areas of several square blocks that could be characterized as immigrant Jewish neighborhoods. Fargo's was next to the Red River; Duluth's was on the West End. All these neighborhoods accommodated a vibrant Jewish life: synagogues, kosher butcher shops and other stores catering to Jewish tastes, socialist meeting halls, and Hebrew schools made life comfortable for the Yiddish-speaking inhabitants.

Despite such urban concentrations, the general pattern of Jewish settlement in the Upper Midwest in the late nineteenth and early twentieth centuries was quite different from that of the East Coast, where Jews gravitated mainly to the cities. Two factors accounted for this difference.

The first was that a significant number of Jews lived in small towns in areas throughout the region. One such area was the Mesabi Iron Range in northern Minnesota. There, by 1905, iron mining replaced logging as the dominant industry and fueled the growth of numerous towns. Seeking economic opportunity, Eastern European Jews settled in Chisholm, Eveleth, Hibbing, and Virginia. These towns all sustained large enough Main Streets to support numerous Jewish stores, and each town had a synagogue. Still smaller Iron Range towns typically had one or two Jewish

A woman stands in front of a typical dwelling on St. Paul's West Side, about 1910. Single homes and duplexes predominated in this neighborhood.

By the 1920s, Hibbing had a substantial Jewish community. Among the numerous merchant families were the Saperos and the Nideses (store marquees, left).

businesses, while Duluth, the premier port of Lake Superior, had the third-largest Jewish population in the Upper Midwest.

A great number of Jews who put down roots on the Iron Range had emigrated from Lithuania, had entered the country through the Great Lakes, and had initially settled in port cities such as Duluth or neighboring Superior, Wisconsin. Family ties between the port cities and the hinterland towns were strong. One sign of this is that no Jewish cemetery was established on the Iron Range until the mid-1950s.

The ethnic composition of non-Jews on the Iron Range was unique to the Upper Midwest. Finns comprised the largest contingent of Northern Europeans among the mineworkers, and they labored alongside Italians and South Slavs. Jews worked to establish good relations with these various ethnic groups. The Schibel family of Virginia found that a generation's sojourn in Finland helped them attract customers who were grateful that they could use their native tongue to transact business. Other Jewish merchants used their knowledge of Russian and Polish to befriend and comprehend their Serb, Croat, and Slovenian patrons.

Jews also ran stores in market towns such as Sioux Falls and Aberdeen, South Dakota; and Fargo, Grand Forks, Bismarck, and Minot, North Dakota—commercial centers that served the hinterlands. The story of Jewish life in all these towns was that of the Twin Cities writ small. In each, synagogues were built and land was set aside for cemeteries. Most of these towns sustained religious personnel through the 1950s. Organizational life, while not so diverse as in the Twin Cities, flourished nonetheless. B'nai Brith, Hadassah (the largest national women's Zionist organization), and local branches of national synagogue sisterhood organizations all gave Jews in small towns a sense of connection with national Jewish life.

The growth of a small-town Jewish population, and its limitations, are epitomized in the story of Leon Salet and his wife, Anna. Salet first peddled his way down the Red River valley from Canada in the 1880s. Deciding that Mankato would be a good place to settle, he opened a store and sent for his wife and children. During the early years, she ran the store and he continued peddling. As the business thrived, he sent for family members and landsleit (Jewish people from the same European town) to help him run it. By 1910, Salet employed Theodore Wolf, who also served as rabbi, shochet (ritual slaughterer), and Hebrew teacher. However, around 1917, he left to open his own store in Sheldon, Iowa. It appears that Salet's other relatives and landsleit followed the same route to financial success. Salet finally entrusted his store to the care of his son, and he and Anna moved in 1917 to St. Paul, where they both became renowned as pillars of Jewish philanthropy. Mankato's Jewish population was never again able to employ a Jewish functionary.

The second factor distinguishing the Upper Midwestern Jewish settlement pattern from the one prevailing on the East Coast was that some Jews chose to become homesteaders. Land ownership, which appealed to poor and unskilled men, denoted not only freedom but also a more ennobling life. Craney Goldman Bellin, whose family left Beresenova, a town near Odessa, in 1905 to settle near Williston, North Dakota, recalled that one of the reasons her father decided to homestead was that a customer in Russia had called him a parasite— for, as a shopkeeper, he produced nothing. Other Jews tried farming because they had grown up in semirural environments in Russia and hated the taste they had gotten of American big-city life.

They were able to satisfy this urge to try farming because homestead land was still available in the Dakotas as late as 1910, although by then the remaining acreage was of marginal productivity. Between 1882 and 1910, about one thousand Jews filed

Hannah Marcus (center), her daughters Rachel Marcus Shapiro and Eda Marcus Schlessinger, and their children in Bowman County, North Dakota, 1910. Hannah and Rachel filed their own homestead claims, while Eda homesteaded with her husband.

homestead claims in North and South Dakota. Jewish women participated, most frequently as wives of homesteaders. But as widows or single women, they were legally able to—and did—stake their own claims. Yet despite the vastness of the landscape, the women

This plat map of a section of Bowman County, in southwestern North Dakota, shows a number of Jewish-owned homesteads.

A Jewish cemetery on the prairie near Ashley, North Dakota

ultimately lived in smaller indoor worlds—typically in twelve-by-fourteen-foot sod or lumber huts.

Many homesteading Jews received aid. Two North Dakota farming colonies were supported by the two Twin Cities Reform congregations. Somewhat later, two national Jewish agricultural societies helped many other settlers. Regardless of whether they received such assistance, most Jewish families gave up farming after less than a decade. The arid plains rarely yielded bountiful crops, and parents worried about how to provide educational and social opportunities for their children.

Although the homesteading experience was short lived for many, it was an invaluable one nonetheless. It stamped those who undertook it as genuine American pioneers. They underwent the full range of settler experiences as they created homes and farms and coped with natural disasters, childbirth, and illness. They found themselves living alongside people who had emigrated from other countries or parts of the United States, and they learned domestic and farming techniques from them. Just as peddling in rural areas had done for so many other Jews, farming imparted some sink-or-swim lessons in how to become Americans. In both occupations, Jews interacted with a variety of people who spoke a medley of languages. Finally, Jewish homesteaders who could sell their land had capital for the next endeavor, which, it was hoped, would be more profitable and less bone-breaking.

The only physical evidence remaining in the 1990s of Jewish agricultural attempts in the late nineteenth and early twentieth centuries are lonely prairie cemeteries and such place names as Jew Flats in Pennington County, South Dakota. Fortunately, some settlers left written and oral accounts of their sodbusting days. They relate experiences that differ widely from those that make up often-told East Coast Jewish settlement stories.

A number of those who left farming moved to villages or small towns near their old homesteads and opened general stores, colloquially known as "Jew stores." Many such establishments were in trading-center towns that were strung like beads along the routes of the Great Northern and Northern Pacific railroads, particularly through North Dakota. In South Dakota from the 1920s to the 1940s, Jews often managed stores for the large, Jewish-owned K and K chain, which was based in Sioux City, Iowa.

Jews played an active role in small-town life and often were appointed to local governing boards. Many found great satisfaction and friendship in this milieu. Raising money for sports teams provided a nondenominational civic outlet. Celia Kamins, recalling how women in Dodge, North Dakota, raised funds for the town's teams by providing dinners for traveling salesmen, concluded, "See, those were things that made life worth living in those little towns, too." Others felt the barriers between themselves and the surrounding Christian community more keenly. Florence Shuman Sher recalled that her mother, Minnie Shuman, "had no social life" in West Union, Iowa, and relied on infrequent trips to relatives in Dubuque for such sustenance.

Jews in small towns kept their religious and cultural ties healthy by traveling to centers with larger Jewish populations to celebrate

religious holidays and visit family members. Sons sometimes boarded with town Jews long enough to prepare for bar mitzvah. Miles
Fiterman of Minneapolis recalled that his parents led a split existence for ten years during the 1930s so that he and his brother could
obtain a Jewish education. His father traveled from Thief River
Falls in northwestern Minnesota to Minneapolis each weekend to
see his wife and sons. Upon completing high school, children raised
in small towns usually went off to college or found work (and community) in cities—and never returned home. Parents often followed
their settled children to the cities.

The variety and fluidity of Jewish settlement within the region, as
well as the problems Jews in small towns faced, are exemplified by
the experiences of Blanche Halpern's large extended family. After
an uncle in Minneapolis helped the family emigrate from Rumania in
1900, some of its members settled there; others, on his advice, went
directly to homesteads in North Dakota. Roughly five years later, a
handful of Minneapolis relatives also tried life on the land. After
farming episodes of relatively short duration, several family members
returned to Minneapolis, while various other Halperns opened stores
in the small North Dakota towns of Hebron, Richardton, and
Belfield. The families fit into small-town life as well as they could, but
the children were not allowed to date non-Jews. This stricture was
typical; understandably, it limited their future in such places. They
traveled to larger towns to celebrate Jewish holidays. By the early
1920s, most of the Dakota Halpern contingent had returned to live
in Minneapolis so that their children could be afforded educational
opportunities and a social life. Interestingly, the eldest Halpern children initially had trouble fitting into the Jewish milieu of the big city.

The wide distribution of Jewish population around the Upper
Midwest, which began in the 1870s with the growth of the railroads
and the availability of homestead lands, reached its peak in the
1920s and began to recede during the Great Depression. In the
Dakotas, as the farmers with whom they traded went broke, Jewish
storeowners, and the small-town Jewish presence in general, closed
up. Many of the merchants resettled in the Twin Cities; others followed the farmers west.

Named locales are discussed in this book.
Dots designate other places where Jews lived in these three states.

MINNESOTA

Thief River
Falls

Virginia
Chisholm   Biwabik
Keewatin   Eveleth
Nashwauk   Hibbing

Moorhead

Duluth
Cloquet   Superior

Nemadji

Brainerd

Hinckley

Ogilvie

St. Cloud

St. Croix
Falls

Osseo   White Bear Lake
Stillwater
Minneapolis   St. Paul

Le Sueur

Mankato

Winona

Wells   Austin
Albert Lea

Era Bell Thompson, 1924

The Iron Range towns retained the bulk of their population until the early 1980s, when the taconite industry declined, forcing iron mines to close. With this development, Jewish merchants folded and followed unemployed miners out of town. Since most of the iron ore was shipped out through Duluth, the Jewish community there also contracted.

Smaller waves of immigrants arrived in the Upper Midwest after World War II. As immigration quotas were eased to allow Displaced Persons to enter the United States, about one thousand of them were settled between 1948 and 1950, predominantly in the Twin Cities. Another group began arriving in the early 1970s from the Soviet Union. At first the Hebrew Immigrant Aid Society (HIAS) acted as a clearinghouse for the new immigrants and assigned Jewish communities all over the United States a certain quota to take care of. Although HIAS was still functioning in the mid-1990s, by that time the desire for family reunification played a major role in determining where immigrants settled. Cumulatively, from 1973 to 1995 about four thousand former Soviet citizens were added to Upper Midwestern Jewish communities.

•

The process of settlement in the region had several main facets: adjusting to the climate and the physical spaces; creating Jewish life and communities, sometimes over great distances; and learning to live among non-Jewish people from a variety of ethnic groups. This process took its course on farms and in the small towns and big cities alike. Jewish farmers learned that their livelihood—indeed, their very lives—frequently depended on having good relations with their neighbors. Some Jews enjoyed their small-town experiences, while others were ambivalent at best. Children, particularly, were the butt of the kind of prejudice that mainly surfaced in the form of name-calling. (It is relevant to bear in mind that all ethnic groups but Old-Stock Americans were subject to slurs in the 1910s and 1920s.) African-American writer and editor Era Bell Thompson recalled her 1920s girlhood in Bismarck, North Dakota, in her autobiography, *American Daughter* (1946). About her friendship with Emily Zvorist

The main street of Cole Harbor, North Dakota, about 1912. Emily Zvorist is second from left.

("Sarah Cohn" in the book), Thompson wrote, "If they called me a coon, they called her a kike," adding that there was no embarrassment when the two friends were together. Furthermore, it was not unusual for different members of the same family to have sharply diverging recollections concerning the anti-Semitism of neighbors. For example, while Rose Rapaport Schwartz recalled little prejudice in Wishek, North Dakota, the town her family moved to after leaving the farm, her sister Laura Rapaport Borsten retorted, "How lucky for you to block it out." The anti-Semitism aimed at children in many small towns generally did not disturb commercial relationships among adults. Jewish merchants by and large were not impeded from earning decent livings in such places. Also, in the Dakotas and on the Iron Range, Catholics were the target of the Ku Klux Klan during the 1920s, while significant numbers of Jews were in the same decade being appointed to public boards and offices.

Jews in St. Paul have customarily had rather harmonious dealings with their non-Jewish neighbors. For example, during the nineteenth century they were welcome to join the city's numerous German-speaking cultural clubs. Some historians ascribe these good relations to the fact that Jews were among the earliest settlers, as well as to the fact that St. Paul had a large Catholic population, which often cooperated with the Jews to counterbalance the powerful Protestant group.

Jews first arrived in Minneapolis in the late 1860s, almost two decades after the city had been founded by Protestant Old-Stock Americans; the population was later augmented by large numbers of Scandinavians. By the 1930s, a superior attitude prevailed among the city's elites and ordinary businesspeople alike that kept Jews from being employed in such fields as insurance and banking, prevented Jewish doctors from obtaining staff positions at hospitals, and thwarted their efforts to join service and private clubs. Jewish women, too, had trouble finding clerical jobs in large firms and were even discouraged from attending business colleges. Jewish schoolteachers were also rare in Minneapolis.

This situation did not begin to improve until the late 1940s. In 1946 journalist Carey McWilliams wrote an article for *Common Ground* magazine in which he labeled Minneapolis the nation's "capitol [*sic*] of anti-Semitism." The article received wide publicity and caused civic leaders considerable embarrassment. A vigorous new mayor, Hubert H. Humphrey, created the Mayor's Council on Human Relations to study discrimination against Jews, blacks, and Asians. The study was made public in 1948, and it resulted in a great deal of civic soul searching as well as in the passage of laws banning job discrimination.

During the same period that their husbands and older children were suffering from discrimination in the workplace and the civic arena, Jewish and non-Jewish women met and to some extent cooperated through organizations such as the National Council of Jewish Women (NCJW), the Woman's Club of Minneapolis, and the League of Women Voters. Female Jewish leaders seem scarcely to have been touched by anti-Semitism: Nina Morais Cohen, a founding member of the NCJW in Minneapolis, was also a founder of the Woman's Club and had strong ties to woman suffrage organizations. Fanny Fliegelman Brin of Minneapolis, a nationally active world-peace advocate in the 1920s and early 1930s and national president of the NCJW in the mid-1930s, worked diligently and effectively to organize a score or more nondenominational women's organizations to participate in the Women's United Nations Rally, a yearly event inaugurated in 1944. It appears that the civic sphere, as represented by the organizations mentioned above as well as by institutions such as Community Chest, was relatively more hospitable to Jewish women than the Rotary and Minneapolis branch of the American Automobile Association were to their husbands. The ways in which anti-Semitism affected relations between Jewish and non-Jewish clubwomen, however, needs greater study.

.

In 1996 the Upper Midwest's roughly forty-five thousand Jews were concentrated in the Twin Cities, with only a few thousand living outside the metropolitan area. They constituted about 2 percent of the Twin Cities' population, 1 percent of Minnesota's population, and an even smaller fraction in the Dakotas. Relatively speaking, they were economically secure and socially accepted. Ironically, the major problem, according to some Jews, seemed to be too much acceptance—if a 50-percent rate of intermarriage could be used as a standard of measurement. The major challenge was to maintain a viable community despite high intermarriage rates and despite outmigration to Sunbelt cities.

As Jews moved both within and out of the Upper Midwest, there was a danger that their unique experiences in the region would be forgotten. Their forebears tried their hand at farming, and for a time they played an important role in the commercial life of almost every small town in the region as shopkeepers and, less frequently, as scrap-metal dealers. In the cities as well, the majority occupied a commercial and trade niche rather than a proletarian one, for there was no large garment industry to employ tens of thousands of workers. These Jews founded institutions to help retain their Judaism. To the extent that they were accepted, they also contributed to the civic life of the communities in which they earned their living. Fitting in while staying separate were the twin tensions under which they lived their lives. The strength of the metropolitan Jewish communities was a testament to their endurance, but their presence on the land and in the small towns was also important. Both kinds of experience were vital to immigrant Jews as they became Jewish Americans.

VOICES

WHY JEWS CHOSE THE UPPER MIDWEST

Most of the first Jews to arrive in the Upper Midwest were from Germany. Sarah Thal, along with her husband, Solomon, and daughter, Elsie, first went to Milwaukee, where her lack of English was no problem in that largely German-speaking city. As she traveled to the rural area that became Nelson County, North Dakota, in the early 1880s, it became a hindrance. Sam Thal was an early real estate investor and sheep rancher in that county.

My brother-in-law, Sam Thal, advised us to go to Dakota Territory. He had been out there and thought highly of the prospects. In fact, he had a large farm out there and only twenty-eight miles from the railroad. My husband was anxious to get started and as soon as he could leave me he went out there. Six weeks later I followed. The only English I knew was "Yes" and "All right," and when my fellow passengers admired my baby and asked, "Is it a girl?" I said "Yes," and when they said "Is it a boy?" I said "Yes." I didn't know why they looked at each other and smiled.

———

Marlchen Deutsch and her family, also from Germany, put down roots in Minneapolis in the 1870s.

[I was born in Karlsruhe, Baden, in 1848.] From there I moved to Davenport, Iowa in 1869. . . . I had relatives there, so that it offered me an *Anfangspunkt* [starting point] to America. I was married there to Mr. Deutsch, and we came to Minneapolis in 1873. We came because we had heard that it was a flourishing town.

———

Fannie Feinstein, a widow with six children, fled Russia in the early 1880s. As her granddaughter Sylvia Feinstein Peilen later told it, remarriage was Fannie's best guarantee of economic survival.

In the days of the pogrom [my mother's father] was injured and died a young man leaving his wife, Fannie, to support six children. American relatives made it possible for passage of them to America in 1883. They landed in New Haven, Connecticut, and lived there for three years. At that time a marriage was arranged between my grandmother Fannie Feinstein with a rabbi of sorts as well as a *shochet* by the name of Goldstein. [They moved to St. Paul.]

———

Women like Marlchen Deutsch appear to have welcomed a new beginning. According to Max and Bella Borow's daughter Pearl Borow Goodman, Bella faced the move west with much trepidation.

My Mother came from a small town outside of Vilna . . . when she met my Father. After they were married, they moved from New York . . . to Bethlehem Pa., then they moved to Philadelphia. . . . My father had a relative in Fargo who constantly wrote and persisted that my Father must come West—it was a young and growing country for a young man. Against my Mother's wishes, my Father went alone and after being there 6 months, he wrote and asked my Mother to come out with the children, and make their home in Fargo [around 1910]. She told me she never cared for Fargo when she arrived there—it was a rugged land—no sidewalks—nothing but mud and more mud.

Laura Rapaport Borsten's father and uncle left Odessa to farm in Argentina in the early 1900s. Their wives had other ideas.

My mother was one independent feminist. She wasn't going to go to Argentina. She had never heard of Argentina. But her family from Bialystock had begun to move to Pittsburgh, and she went down and changed the tickets [they had bought so that their wives could join them], and she and her sister-in-law headed for America . . . and my father and [uncle] Felix could do nothing except just leave Argentina and come up and join their rebellious wives. . . . My father hated Pittsburgh, having lived his whole life in a shtetl. . . . He was part of a group of Jews rounded up by the Jewish Agricultural Society to take land on the border of the Dakotas.

———

Charles Losk left Russia in 1905. Forty-two years later he wrote about the arduous journey to the Upper Midwest.

The reason we came to Anamoose, N.Dak., is because we had 2 neighbors [German farmers] from Europe . . . with whom we corresponded . . . and they kept us informed about the homestead laws . . . and we decided even before we left Europe to come to North Dakota and take up homesteads.

———

Economic opportunity and friends or relatives who have already put down roots are still key attractions for anyone thinking of settling in the Upper Midwest. In 1988 Jane Sinitsky and her family left Leningrad for St. Paul.

I had a very close friend. . . . We wrote to each other all the time. She just told me, "Come here. It's a nice place." . . . She married a man from North Dakota. She found a Jew in North Dakota!

ACCOUNTS OF TRAVEL

Amelia Ullmann's story of her trip up the Mississippi serves as a vivid reminder that, in 1855, the heart of America had not yet been transformed by industrialization.

The little settlements became fewer and fewer the further northward that we went; cultivated fields . . . disappeared; even the settler's hut was no longer visible. . . . Bunches of trees began to dot the landscape and then forests rolled down over the bluffs to the river's edge. It was a forest, too, primeval . . . vines grew luxuriant[,] binding together the giant trees. . . . [S]ometimes a deer broke through the tangle of vegetation and slaked his thirst at the edge of the river or the shriek of a wild cat came from the depth of the woods. . . . The savagery of the scene and the length and tediousness of the journey had a depressing effect upon me.

————

Sarah Thal's description of her westward journey from Milwaukee to the northern part of Dakota Territory in the 1880s is rich in detailing travel difficulties and the Dakota landscape, which typically had a startling effect on Europeans. By then trains had superseded riverboats as the main mode of transportation.

At St. Paul I changed trains. Here I sat my baby down. She followed a woman who had a cage of white rats. I managed to find her, just in time to catch my train. We reached Grand Forks late at night. Being unable to speak English, I could not make my wants known so I went to bed without supper. . . . I reached Larimore hungry but safely. Here I met my husband. He was wearing a buffalo skin coat, the first I had ever seen. . . . I had never ridden in a wagon. . . . I climbed upon the seat, wrapped my baby in [a] shawl and drove off into the unbroken prairies. The road was a rude wagon trail. Here and there we passed a sod cabin or shanty and saw a patch of plowed ground. . . . Toward dark our team lost the road and we drove into a buffalo hole and upset the wagon. . . . The horses had unhitched themselves. My husband was holding

Train depot, Wilton, North
Dakota, about 1920

the lines and was obliged to follow them home as they hurried
across the prairie.

We could see a light in the distance which we believed was
Harrisburg. Mr. Mendelson was so nearsighted that I was obliged
to lead the way. I carried my baby. We found ourselves back at
our starting place three times; it was after midnight when we
finally reached Harrisburg. Here we found an escort with a
lantern who saw us home. Everyone was in bed so I was obliged
to go to bed hungry once more.*

———

*The Mr. Mendelson mentioned was probably a land speculator who tried to
develop the town of Wamduska on Stump Lake, hoping the Great Northern
Railroad would intersect there. Instead it crossed at Devils Lake, to the north.

The Losk extended family emigrated from Odessa in 1905. Their journey, as Charles Losk described it, began at the Black Sea and ended in Anamoose, North Dakota.

In these 5 weeks we traveled through 5 different countries: Russia—Poland—Lithuania—Germany—England and stopped and went by perhaps 5000 cities—towns—and villages—and crossed perhaps 1000 rivers and small streams. And crossed the Baltic Sea and the North Sea—the Kiel Canal and the [Atlantic] Ocean—and many thousands of miles of railroad travel in Europe and the U.S.A. . . . It was a hardship on all of us, especially the women and the children.

———

The Tenenbaums, consisting of a mother and five children, traveled in 1905 from Lithuania across the North Sea to Liverpool. There, as Morris Tenenbaum related, they were assisted by a Jewish Travelers Aid Society, then sailed the Atlantic and traveled up the St. Lawrence River.

A Jewish man from the Travelers Aid . . . Society suggested that we could wait on the railroad platform near our baggage. . . . We crossed the Atlantic Ocean in six and one-half days. . . . We encountered no difficulty at the Port of Entry in Montreal. We were instructed how to get on the correct train to Chicago, . . . where we changed trains for St. Paul, Minn.—to end our travels for many years and to start a NEW LIFE for each of us. At the Union Station in St. Paul we were met by Father, who had borrowed a horse and a junk wagon in which to transport us and our bundles of luggage.

FIRST IMPRESSIONS

Amelia Ullmann's impressions of the St. Paul of 1855 depict a town that was almost totally dependent upon the river for the transporting of people and merchandise.

A low marshy track lay upon the right[,] covered over with tall swamp grass and . . . ponds coated with green scum. The land rose back of this. . . . Within the elevated space between . . . two ridges was St. Paul. A few wooden shanties were scattered along the foot of the [ridge] we passed and upon the higher land further on were the more pretentious buildings that made up the town. The landing was the river bank leveled for a hundred feet or more and the swamp filled in with piles driven into the water at the edge to fasten the boat ropes. Stacks of merchandise were piled upon the river bank and a crowd of people were lounging about awaiting the arrival of the boat. The boat's whistle was to St. Paul then as to most of the towns on the river a signal for a general rush to the landing.

———

Sophie Turnoy arrived in America in 1908 with her mother and brothers. They had come from Seltz, a Russian-Polish shtetl, to join her father who was homesteading near Wilton, North Dakota. He had left Russia after a pogrom four years earlier, determined to build a more secure life for his family. Sophie described her first impressions of the landscape around Wilton.

St. Paul's lower levee, where new settlers arrived, about 1865

I remember looking out upon the endless prairies. The road that stretched ahead was made by the wheels of wagons such as my father's. . . . It ran through the steel gray grass that covered the rolling hills and valleys. There was hardly a quarter mile of level ground. The hills rolled on, one after the other—all sizes, all shapes, all heights. Some hills seemed so tall that we wondered how we could make it safely down the steep descent. . . . We traveled all day, and I don't remember meeting any other wagon or stopping anywhere. There were no houses or trees or rivers, only prairies and hills and sky. . . . Finally, we saw the farm. The wheat had been harvested. . . . Along each field lay piles of rocks in heaps; each rock had been dug out of the surface of the earth and carried or rolled to make these heaps. The cleared fields seemed to be swallowed up in the vast land that stretched endlessly in all directions.

———

Rachel Bella Kahn was born in the Ukraine and orphaned at an early age. In 1894 she entered into an arranged marriage with the Russian-born Abraham Calof, a homesteader near Devils Lake, North Dakota. Their early years together were filled with hardship.

This was my first sight of what awaited me as a pioneer woman. The furniture consisted of a bed, a rough table made of wood slats, and two benches. The place was divided up into two sections, the other being the kitchen which held a stove and beside it a heap of dried cow dung.* When I inquired about this, I was told that this was the only fuel this household had. . . . I silently vowed that my home would be heated by firewood and that no animal waste would litter my floor. How little I knew. How innocent I was.

———

The Minenberg family—father, mother, and four-year-old Rachel—left New York City for North Dakota in 1907 as part of

*Animal waste was often used for fuel on the treeless prairie.

a group of sixty families sent by the Jewish Agricultural Society. They arrived in Ashley and soon commenced farming a dozen miles from town.

[Our first house] was a little wooden shack with a tar paper roof and behind it one of those coffin shaped buttes sometimes seen on the prairie. This shack was to be our home.

It stood with its back to the butte which rose perhaps a quarter of a mile away. It was a house such as a child might have drawn, with two window[s] and at one side a door. It had a small tin chimney tied to the roof with wires. Inside it had a bed in one corner, in the other corner a black iron stove for cooking and for heat. Near the bed stood a tall black clothes closet on legs, and between the two windows a table with a lamp. We had no chairs. My mother sat on a sack of potatoes, my father on a sack of flour, and I on a wooden box father had brought from town. . . . My mother looked out, saw no other human habitation. She had been brought up in a city. She was terrified.

———

Betty Rosenberg, who had lived in Chicago with her parents, met her husband-to-be at a resort in Indiana; they married in 1915.

My impression of Beach [North Dakota, near the Montana border] when the train pulled in the middle of the town's business section, coming from Chicago, was far from favorable. I saw nine grain elevators on one side of the street, a few old frame buildings, the leading stores. . . . It was all primitive to a city girl, no plumbing[;] we had to pump water from a well at 40 to 50 below zero, a hardship for me. I did not let my parents know.

———

Kopple Hallock's is one the few available descriptions by Jews of a raucous Iron Range town. His parents, Charles and Etta, were born in Lithuania and met and married in Duluth. They soon moved to Hibbing to open a clothing store.

Grain elevators dominate the skyline and line the railroad tracks of Ashley, North Dakota, about 1920.

When Dad and Mother came to Hibbing in 1900 . . . there were 57 saloons in town. With this number, you might think that this was the main industry. [That], however, was logging. It was some time later that iron ore mining became the leading industry.

———

Newly arrived on the West Side of St. Paul in 1913 and looking for work, nineteen-year-old Sam Char, born in Warsaw, was used to paved streets.

I got some breakfast and went out to see where I was. The West Side did not make a good impression on me. There were no sidewalks and the street was not paved and there was mud all over.

———

In her slightly fictionalized family history, They Were Strangers *(1995), Slovie Solomon Apple recalled her mother's tales of arriving*

The intersection of Sixth Street North and Lyndale Avenue on Minneapolis's North Side was the hub of the city's Jewish community in the 1920s. Note S. Brochin Delicatessen at left.

on the North Side of Minneapolis. Clara, her mother, had come from a shtetl in Rumania and was unused to such bustle.

That was a place noisy with the voices of bustling housewives and crying children. Other children played on the streets and sidewalks. There were the sounds of peddlers calling out their wares, wooing the women to come out and buy. Both sides of the streets were lined with little shops. . . . This was a large Jewish community! Big signs and little signs, some with big Yiddish letters and others with small letters, hung crookedly in front of shops . . . [that] were small, crowded tightly, one next to the other.

———

Although immigrants received letters telling them what to expect, there was always a shock once they arrived. Galina Khaikina Dreytser and her family traveled to St. Paul from Leningrad in 1989.

We were so exhausted because of a very long way from Rome to New York City. Eugene was one year old and he didn't sleep all night. . . . I was very surprised because I imagined America like Manhattan . . . a lot of skyscrapers, but when I saw a lot of little, little houses, . . . I said, "It's a village, it's not America." I didn't know that America had one-floor houses.

THE IMPORTANCE OF NEIGHBORS

The Mill family—father Israel and sons Manacha and Max— farmed from about 1890 to 1919 near Edmore, North Dakota. Israel's granddaughter Rose Mill Sweed recounted their early experiences on the prairie.

The neighbors taught them to build the thick walls of sod, roofs of stalks of grain interwoven with ropes made of tree bark, and the floor of sand found near river banks and sloughs. Adjoining the outside of the north wall of the house was the chicken coop with rows of wooden strips for the chickens to roost on. The coop served as insulation from the bitter cold northern winds in the winter. The one room sod house served as a combination living room, bedroom, and kitchen. The outer walls and adjoining chicken coop were banked with mud and in the winter with manure to keep out the bitter cold wind.[*]

Bessie Halpern left her home in Minneapolis in 1907 to try homesteading in North Dakota, along with her fiancé and members of her extended family.

[*]Sweed here described the first prairie dwelling her grandfather built. The technique is typical of that used in German-Russian farm dwellings.

On the Homestead, for recreation, were the country dances; we went and returned on the hay racks, returning early in the morning. Before returning home, we had breakfast with the cowboys—they were the cooks, making pancakes with unwashed hands. I was even frightened of the cowboys with their pistols. They talked and spit as fast as they used the guns—fast, and me from a city, how I was upset.

———

Sarah Thal's second child was born in the early 1880s under typically trying circumstances.

That same Fall my second baby, Jacob, was born. I was attended by a Mrs. Saunders, an English woman. We couldn't understand each other. It was in September. The weather turned cold and the wind blew from the north. . . . I was so cold that during the first night they moved my bed into the living room by the stove and pinned sheets around it to keep the draft out and so I lived

North Dakota homesteader Bessie Schwartz (left) and several members of her family outside her sod hut, about 1890. Homestead dwellings were often situated at a corner of the property so that neighbors could be closer to each other.

through the first child birth in the prairies. I like to think that God watched out for us poor lonely women when the stork came.

————

From the 1870s to the late 1880s, the Phillips family home-steaded first outside Moorhead, Minnesota, and then across the Red River near Fargo, North Dakota. When Hannah was about to give birth, she received help from an unexpected source, according to the family story recounted by grandchild Henry Fine.

When my aunt Sarah was born, my grandfather was away peddling. The rain had cut a hole in the roof of the sod farmhouse, and my grandmother was about to give birth to her fifth child. She was in pain and obviously suffering. My mother remembered the scene well. All of a sudden two Indians appeared in the house. They looked at my grandmother, saw the condition she was in, and without saying a word turned and walked out. Within ten minutes two squaws were in the house, and they delivered my aunt Sarah. They never knew where those Indians came from, but after that my grandmother insisted on moving off the farm.

————

By the mid-1880s Sarah Thal had mastered English sufficiently to exchange domestic lore with neighbors.

At about this time I had made the acquaintance of Mrs. Stratton. She wove rag carpets, three yards for fifty cents. . . . She would take faded colorless rags and dye them bright colors and weave them into gay patterns. . . . From her I learned to make citron and green tomato pickles and cakes and pies, and in turn I taught my neighbors how to make coffee cake, potato salad, cottage cheese, noodles, etc.

————

Rose Rapaport Schwartz's family farmed from about 1905 to 1915 in an area of North Dakota where many non-Jewish German-Russians, as well as Jews, lived.

The Jewish Community was very clannish and really brought their shtetl life with them to North Dakota. I know they had many get togethers, with people doing amateur plays and readings. . . . I remember vaguely incidents having to do with gentiles and how hard it was for them (our parents) to accept a kindness from them. . . . They learned to make cheeses, how to winterize vegetables, store eggs, and so forth from [the gentiles] but were always afraid a little.

————

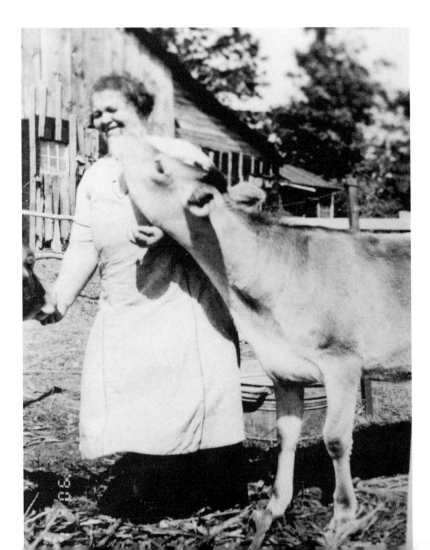

Rachael Freedland being nuzzled by a calf on the family farm near Osseo, Minnesota, about 1915

The Freedland family had a dairy farm near Osseo, Minnesota, from 1913 through World War I. It was close enough to Minneapolis for Morris's father to sell his sour cream and cottage cheese on the North Side twice a week, weather permitting.

Once we were snowed in for ten days by a blizzard. After a few days we ran out of bread, and my mother sent me over to the Olsons on skis to see if any flour was available. Mrs. Olson had me come in to thaw out, and . . . said, "We are out of flour too, but here are some potatoes. Tell your mother to make potato pancakes." So I took home the small sack of potatoes and for the next few days we had potato pancakes. They didn't taste as good as bread would have, but they were a welcome treat for our empty stomachs.

CREATING NEW HOMES

Rachel Kahn Calof recounted her efforts in 1895 and 1896 to forge a home out of a wooden shack.

I prepared a pile of clay and began to knead it with my feet. . . . I worked the moistened clay onto the walls, between the slats, making a smooth inner finish over the rough boards. Finishing, I surveyed the result. A miracle had taken place. Our rude shanty had become a palace. . . . I whitewashed the walls and made fine curtains for the windows from flour sacks.

———

From 1905 to 1910, the Wrottenberg family lived in a prairie home that daughter Jeanette later described.

The first home I remember was a three-room sod house on the North Dakota prairie. The roof, which stood but a few feet above ground, was thatched with sod. . . . [O]ur resourceful young mother . . . papered . . . the walls five layers deep with flamboyant posters left behind by a traveling circus.

———

Ethel Schlasinger Overby wrote her family story in the third person. Her parents emigrated from Odessa in 1906 and began homesteading near Ashley, North Dakota.

[Sarah] designed furniture for their home, and Noah built it from rough lumber recycled from dry-goods shipping boxes. . . . Her greatest success was the sofa, a box that provided comfortable pillowed seating and also a concealed storage space. . . . Sarah bought flowered cretonne and made fringe-trimmed curtains and a sofa cover. She painstakingly painted the wooden floor to look like the parquet floors of Odessa.

———

Rachel Minenberg Baker described the cozy home created in a sod hut near Ashley, North Dakota, in about 1908.

A sod house, made from blocks of black earth cut from the soil[,] each block being somewhat larger than a shoe box. . . . The windows, when they are set into these deep walls, look almost like tunnels. The Weisburd house, which had two rooms, was whitewashed inside and out. It was warm in winter and incredibly cool in summer. I remember one room, filled with three beds, each one piled high with immaculate white featherbeds. The other room had the usual cooking stove and table covered with a piece of white oil cloth. It was lit of course by a kerosene lamp.

HARDSHIPS AND TRAGEDIES

Children's illnesses assumed frightening proportions on the prairie, where help was usually far away. Often children became ill during the worst weather, when it was impossible to travel. In 1896 Rachel Kahn Calof was the mother of a one-year-old.

Without warning, little Minnie was suddenly stricken with a violent illness. . . . To summon and bring the doctor would take two or three days, and in any event his fee to come to our area would be seventy-five dollars. . . . [This was far] beyond our means. . . . Incapable of hindering decline . . . my mind chose to deal with the actualities which would follow. Where would I find a white sheet in which to wrap her little body? And how would she be buried? I recalled the many stories I had been told of how the prairie wolves (people who knew called them "the butchers") on the day following burial on the open plain would pull the body from the grave and feed on the flesh and bones.*

———

Natural disasters leading to death were all too common on the open prairie, where there was nothing to stop the wind from blowing the blinding snow in winter. Sarah Thal recounted just such an early experience.

About six weeks after my arrival, I experienced our first real blizzard, a true Nor-wester. The Seliger's [sic] cabin [they were close neighbors and Jews] was so poorly built they were afraid to spend the night there. Mr. Seliger came to our place and asked if he might have the team to bring his wife and baby. The storm was such that a team couldn't have found its way. My husband advised him to keep to the plowed ground which ran from his door to ours. He reached home and started out with his family. He was obliged to let go of them for just a bit and he lost them. Late at night he came to our place almost frozen. He had been searching for his wife and baby since mid-afternoon. The storm lasted three days.

During that time no one ventured from the house and when it cleared mother and baby were found about fifty feet from their house, of course frozen to death. Their bodies were taken to their cabin and word was sent to the nearest settlement by Mr. Buzzard, a lawyer from Larimore. A few days later a sleigh full of men and women came from somewhere. We heated water and thawed the bodies sufficiently to fit them in a home made coffin. They were buried on the homesite and, as I couldn't speak

*Minnie survived her illness.

English, I never learned who those kind people were or where they came from. I remember that beautiful baby to this day. She wore coral earrings and necklace. The frost glistened on her cheeks making her look more like a wax doll than a once live baby.

———

The plains could be dangerous in summer as well. Rose Mill Sweed recounted a tragedy that unfolded near her family's Edmore, North Dakota, homestead.

When a prairie fire broke out, as they often did during the hot dry weather, the neighbors all joined in to fight it. One young woman whose husband had gone to help fight the fires, being busy with her household chores, failed to see the fire surrounding her cabin, because the wind had shifted to a different direction. Looking out the open door she suddenly realized the danger and became terribly frightened and she started to run through the prairie to her nearest neighbor a mile or two away. But in her fright she became confused and ran in the wrong direction right into the midst of the fire. When the neighbors found her a couple of hours later, she was burned almost beyond recognition. Hers was the first grave in the newly formed [Jewish] cemetery which was set aside by the county. . . . [The cemetery was located] in the midst of the prairie high on a hill.

———

Some wives who came to farms found that life unendurable and left, for varying periods. The Labovich family, consisting of five men and their wives, left Rumania and homesteaded in the area near the Souris River, in what is now northeastern North Dakota, in 1888. Anna Labovich Rosen recalled an aunt's experiences.

Aunt Kate was married before she was sixteen and she buried two children on the farm. When she became pregnant with Frank, she prevailed upon Uncle Israel to allow her to go to her brother who lived in New York. After Frank was born she refused to

Sam and Inez Cheit on a winter day in Hague, North Dakota, 1922

come back to the farm and she told Uncle unless he sold the farm she would not return. She lived in New York for 11 years and finally came back.

———

The Handelmans first settled in Chicago in the late 1890s. About 1904, the family joined a grandfather and uncle homesteading about twenty miles east of Wilton, North Dakota, as son Leo recalled.

The first winter the settlers got a taste of what was in store for them. Two to three feet of snow covered the plains, and drifts as

Lena Leiderscheider hung her parents' pictures on the walls before her wedding in North Dakota in 1918. She wanted them to be present, at least symbolically.

high as 15 feet were common. The temperature dropped as low as 45 degrees below zero at times. . . . Many of the settlers were already concluding that this life was just too hard and were making plans to return to Chicago. . . . However, my father harbored no such defeatist ideas. . . . My mother, on the other hand, could not cope with the hardships.

The change from a sheltered and comfortable life in Rumania, to one of hardship and loneliness was more than she could bear. My father saw that she was approaching a nervous breakdown, so he sent her back again to her parents in Rumania. There she gradually recovered but, of course, she was very lonesome and longed for the family.

My father was left on the farm with my sisters Frieda, Minette, Shirley and myself. And it now became necessary for my oldest sister Frieda to take care of the family. What a frightful and impossible job for a girl of 14, especially in such an unfavorable environment.

———

Rachel Minenberg Baker remembered how her family survived the elements, thanks to the aid of neighbors and the actions of her mother.

We had several adventures when we were alone on the farm. One day a tornado came. I saw the clouds coiling like a black snake in the sky. Then the cloud dipped like a funnel toward the ground.

Mother and I ran inside. She closed the window. We felt a dreadful roar directly over our heads. Then suddenly the roof was lifted off, and rain came pouring down on us in such torrents that objects in the room began to bob and swim.

Mother thrust my brother and me into the clothes closet to keep us from drowning. She stood on a box near the closet holding up the baby in her arms. When the storm passed, she opened the door to let the water out. Then she dragged our bed clothes out to dry on the prairie suddenly blazing in the hot sun.

After a while we heard wagon wheels and from many directions fellow farmers appeared. They found our roof in pieces but with hammer and nails they put it on again before night. . . .

The tornado took place in the spring. The following summer we had a prairie fire. One morning we saw smoke on the horizon. Above us the sky took on a strange coppery tone. Then in the distance we saw the fire racing in a low line along the horizon.

My mother did not know that a prairie fire travels too fast to do more than singe the foundations of a shack. It cannot set the shack on fire. She became terrified. With my baby brother in her arms and with me clinging frightened to her leg, she climbed a hill about a half mile from our house and there she began to scream for help. The fire raced into a slough, a low place where the dry grass was very tall. The fire leaped up in high flames. My mother weeping began to call for God to help her.

Then we heard buggy wheels and a buggy appeared at the side of the hill not yet touched by the fire. It was one of our neighbors. He had been sent to reassure my mother and had heard her cries. He rescued us, took us in the buggy to our nearest neighbor, the widow Weisburd, who lived in a sod house. When we got there the house was empty. Everyone had gone off to fight the fire, some to make a [firebreak] by burning a path over which the fire could not jump, other[s] to beat out the flames with gunny sacks dipped in buckets of water.

The man who had rescued us went off to help the others. My mother, afraid to stay in the house took us out into the yard where she found an underground chicken coop dug into the side of the earth which she felt would be safe. We all went in there until the fire had passed crackling over our heads. We came out covered with chicken lice. But fortunately they did not like people and they soon dropped off.

When the people came back from fighting the fire many had singed eyebrows and scorched garments. I can still remember the smell and the excitement as everyone sat around in the sod house drinking innumerable glasses of tea and repeating their exciting stories. Late that afternoon, when we were driven back to our shack, a black prairie stretched under the sky. Only here and there showed white stones, as if from a mammoth, lonely graveyard.

CHAPTER THREE

"And Prairie Dogs Weren't Kosher"
Domestic Life

To me the greatest dignity a Jewish woman can attain is to be the presiding genius in a traditional Jewish home. Every other occupation is "vochedig" [mundane] compared to that. The woman is not a mere housekeeper but the priestess of a "mikdash me'at," a miniature sanctuary, when she conducts a truly Jewish home.
—Sarah Cohen Berman, about 1943

[My parents] got tired of eating potatoes, and prairie dogs weren't kosher.
—Isadore Pitts, about 1913

DEPENDING ON HER circumstances, the traditionally oriented Jewish woman in the Upper Midwest could be cognizant of her exalted role, as Minneapolitan Sarah Cohen Berman was, or worn down by the drudgery of South Dakota homestead life, as Isadore Pitts's parents were. This is as true in the 1990s as it was when Jews began settling in the region one hundred fifty years ago. Whatever the case, the Jewish woman's domestic life centered on raising children who were mindful of their obligations to family and community as well as on keeping a kosher home—one that could be compared to a "miniature sanctuary."

Keeping kosher meant subscribing to a vast store of religious laws and customs. But in America—and particularly in the Upper Midwest—location, level of devotion, and financial means dictated a wide range of observance. Whether the Jewish woman believed that maintaining a kosher home was a sacred mandate or an outmoded custom, the law and lore of kashrut stood as an important link with the past. The frequency with which kashrut arises in written accounts and oral histories attests to the discomfort women felt about tampering with it.

The Hebrew word *kosher* means "fit" or "proper." Most commonly, it refers to Jewish dietary laws. *Kashrut* is the act of keeping kosher. The opposite of kosher is *treyf,* or unfit. The concept stems from several biblical injunctions, the best known of which is "Thou shalt not seethe a kid in its mother's milk," which appears in the books of Exodus and Deuteronomy. Beginning in ancient Israel, this dictate was interpreted to mean that no meat products, including poultry, should ever come in direct contact with any dairy products. Questions involving adherence to kashrut have been discussed and resolved by rabbis through the centuries down to our own day.

Only certain animals are considered fit to eat. Included in this group are quadrupeds that chew their cud and have cloven hooves (cattle, sheep, goats), birds that do not hunt, and fish that have scales and fins. Thus Jews who keep kosher do not eat pork or shellfish, nor do they hunt.

For the observant housewife, keeping kosher entails constant vigilance. Utensils, dishes, cutlery, and dishtowels must be kept in separate drawers or shelves. A fleishig (meat) spoon cannot stir a milchig (milk) pot. (A cream soup spattering into a meat stew would render the latter *treyf.*) Meat and milk are not to mix even in one's stomach: A certain number of hours must pass after eating meat before one is allowed to consume milk products—and vice versa.

Keeping kosher has one other important ramification. The Book of Leviticus includes a prohibition against the consumption of blood, which is the rationale for the kosher slaughter of meat. The animal is supposed to be killed as quickly and painlessly as possible, and its blood is to be drained away. Only a pious, properly trained shochet (slaughterer) may perform this ritual. Even so, only certain portions of the animal are considered kosher;* the rest is sold to non-Jews.

The housewife's responsibility continues after the meat is bought. She might need to remove still more of its blood. This is done by soaking the meat in water, draining it, covering it with coarse "kosher" salt, and finally washing it again.

All of these steps are taken because the Torah (the first five books of the Hebrew Bible) connects food and the act of eating to the concept of holiness. That is why a housewife like Sarah Cohen Berman could consider herself a priestess whose job it was to ensure holiness within the home by observing these rules. Keeping kosher was also a way of differentiating Jews from the peoples among whom

---

*For instance, the loin portion, which contains the tenderest meat, is not kosher unless the sciatic vein is removed.

they settled: A Jew's refusal to eat *treyf* helped ensure that no undue mixing would occur.

When Jews lived in ghettos and compact communities in Europe, keeping kosher was the norm. But in America, a place of apparently limitless freedom of religious expression, women and men could choose which of their traditions would make the transatlantic crossing with them. Would Jewish women continue to maintain kashrut in their homes, or would they discard it as they typically did the sheitel (wig)?

The outcome depended on timing, where one lived, and one's level of religious devotion. Amelia Ullmann, who in 1855 arrived in a St. Paul that received supplies only when the Mississippi River was navigable, learned to eat whatever was available. In her memoirs she noted the monotony of the winter diet, when pork was the only meat to be had. Sarah Thal shuddered at the idea of even cooking pork, but her isolation in the 1880s on a farm in present-day North Dakota led her to discard dietary laws. It was probably true for both women that the scarcity of fresh food in any form militated against mortifying the flesh by attempting to keep kosher. Indeed, according to religious law, maintaining good health is more important than maintaining kashrut.

Kashrut was uppermost in the minds of the founders of St. Paul's Mount Zion Hebrew Association, the first synagogue in the region; for one of their first acts after forming in 1856 was to employ a shochet. By the mid-1870s, however, the position was dropped. This was a sign that the synagogue had moved into Reform Judaism, whose proponents viewed the religion as subject to change and insisted on discarding certain "antiquated" Jewish laws and interpreting others in a more liberal way. The new emphasis of the Reform movement certainly made its precepts more compatible with American life than the demands of traditional Judaism.

For Reform-minded women this emphasis meant that keeping kosher was no longer a necessity. Instead they were encouraged to proclaim their piety by regular synagogue attendance and through organized acts of benevolence. Although Reform Jews led the trend in abandoning kashrut, it was not jettisoned overnight nor even in

a generation. Some German-Jewish women retained elements of keeping kosher, perhaps out of respect for the mothers who had taught them. Culinary habits, in any case, change slowly.

By the late 1910s, however, Upper Midwestern Reform women, through their synagogue auxiliaries, were participating in a development that emphasized their distance from traditional dietary customs. To raise funds for their synagogues, they published cookbooks containing few traditional Jewish recipes but so many non-kosher ones that they formed a genre that folklorist Barbara Kirshenblatt-Gimblett has aptly termed *treyf* cookbooks. The cookbooks mark the assimilation of German Jews into American life, they reflect class aspirations, and they make clear the gap between these well-established Jews and their more recently arrived Eastern European coreligionists. The outside world tended to view Jews as a unified group, which rankled the German Jews. They strove to maintain the differentiations by moving to other neighborhoods, by creating different modes of worship, and, as the cookbooks indicate, by announcing that foods formerly off-limits were now fit to eat.

The Eastern European Jews had begun settling in the Upper Midwest's cities in the two decades before the turn of the century. These women kept kosher strictly. They had come from a part of the world where the whole ethnic culture worked to sustain kashrut. There was no reason not to continue observing it in the Jewish neighborhoods of the region's cities, where, by the time a congregation was formed, kosher meat could be had at affordable prices. (Strikes, such as those in New York City in 1902 and 1917 in which women joined in boycotts to protest the soaring price of kosher meat, seem not to have occurred in the Upper Midwest.) Even smaller towns, such as those on Minnesota's Iron Range, supported shochets until the 1920s. Problems would arise when the kosher butcher moved to a city or decided to cater to the larger gentile trade or when the women began making kashrut a personal choice rather than accepting it as an abiding mandate.

Neighborhood children outside a kosher grocery store at Sixth Avenue North and Lyndale Avenue on Minneapolis's North Side, about 1909

Jews who lived in small towns or on farms in the Dakotas faced more severe circumstances; for them, kosher meat was not readily available. Sent from large cities by nonrefrigerated train, it often arrived in a decomposed state. Farming families, many of whom lived far from railroad stops, faced even more daunting challenges. Circuit-riding rabbis and shochets sometimes helped solve the problem by arriving to slaughter poultry and a steer for each family in the fall of the year; the northern winters kept the meat frozen.

Some women, especially in rural areas, chose to cordon off tradition and maintain what were, in effect, semi-kosher homes. They might reserve certain pots for cooking non-kosher foods, such as the game shot by their husbands or children. Even when they cooked game for their families, though, they generally refused to eat it. It appears that, in general, women were more likely than men to continue keeping kosher. Children may have grown up internalizing some form of double standard.

In time, the strain of coping with such privations as shipments of spoiled meat wore away the resolve of many women living in small towns. The shift was not confined to these locales, however. By the 1930s, when a generation of American-born Jews had come of age, it was clear that keeping kosher was falling into disfavor among the majority of women in the region's small towns and large cities alike. In his 1949 study, *Jews in Transition,* based on research conducted from 1930 to 1946, Rabbi Albert I. Gordon wrote that by the end of World War II no more than 20 percent of Jews in Minneapolis consumed kosher meat. The trend was national as well. Marshall Sklare and Joseph Greenblum's 1967 study of Jewish life in a Chicago suburb, *Jewish Identity on the Suburban Frontier,* found that about 5 percent of second- and third-generation American Jews kept kosher.

Women often cited cost when justifying the switch. More frequently, however, they used the same argument that the Reform movement had made: There were more important ways for the Jewish woman to express religiosity than through what was disparagingly termed "kitchen Judaism." She could, for example, practice

Natalie Chanen Goldstein (left) and Faye Chanen Garelick (foreground) preparing for a Sabbath dinner in their mother Sadie's Minneapolis kitchen, early 1950s

philanthropy and study religious texts. The priestess was beginning to serve at different altars.

.

Women may have enlarged their religious sphere, but one of their most important duties continued to be preparing for home-centered holidays. The three most likely to be observed were the Sabbath, Passover, and Chanukah.*

Women usher in the Sabbath, like all holidays, by lighting candles

*Rosh Hashanah, the Jewish New Year, is certainly a major holiday. But it is synagogue-oriented, and the foods associated with it are rather similar to those of the Sabbath.

and reciting special prayers. Their customary preparations included cleaning both house and children and making special foods so that this holiday could indeed be a foretaste of paradise, a day apart from the rest of the week. In the Upper Midwest earlier in the century even non-Jews took notice, although they may not have understood the meaning. "On Fridays candles burned when the sun went down, and new and mysterious dishes appeared," recalled African-American writer and editor Era Bell Thompson about the Sabbath preparations of her Jewish friend Emily Zvorist's mother in Bismarck, North Dakota, in the 1920s.

Jewish women may have continued to light the candles and serve the traditional dishes in America, but there were changes, attributable to the new environment. By the 1920s, the individualistic, commerce-oriented milieu of the new land led many Jewish storeowners on New York City's Lower East Side, whose clientele was almost all Jewish, to flout the injunction against working on the Sabbath by staying open Friday night and Saturday. Storeowners in the Upper Midwest were every bit as likely to keep their doors open during the Sabbath in order to accommodate their non-Jewish farming and mining customers' shopping habits. Even in the cities, Jews were torn between observing the Sabbath properly by abstaining from labor of any kind and earning a living. Compromises were made in which candles were lit and blessings recited, but father returned to tending the store. The Sabbath, in effect, was turned over to women and children.

The same development had taken place, on a larger scale, among German Jews. As early as the mid-1880s, American founders of the Reform movement altered Sabbath observance significantly by creating a Friday-night service. Although early evidence for the Upper Midwest is scant, by the 1920s this service was in place in both Reform and Conservative synagogues. A short service catering to spiritual needs was followed by refreshments and a chat with friends. Rabbis endeavored to make the synagogue the place to go after dinner on Friday. Still, symphony night and high school sports events competed for "free" weekend time. Although each generation pays lip service to a revival of the traditional twenty-four-hour period of withdrawal from daily life, the occurrence of a major holiday once a week appears to be too much of a good thing for most American Jews to deal with.

Passover and Chanukah, which both come once a year, are holidays still observed by most American Jews in the 1990s. Passover celebrates the liberation of the Children of Israel from bondage in ancient Egypt. The eight-day-long holiday begins with the Seder, the

Gordon family Seder, St. Paul, about 1950

great feast during which the freedom story is retold. For observant women, however, Passover really starts several weeks earlier with a methodical housecleaning. Indeed, the house is to be cleaned so thoroughly that not even a stray bread crumb remains. After that, all the everyday kitchen utensils and dishes are to be replaced on the freshly scrubbed shelves with ones used solely during Passover. Nearer to the holiday, all foods have to be replaced with ones certified kosher for Passover, and all leavening (yeast, baking powder, and baking soda) must be removed from the house. Special foods must then be purchased and prepared. Also, new clothes and shoes are often bought for the holiday, adding yet one more task for the housewife. Getting ready for the festival of freedom is often such a strenuous process that women are exhausted before the Seder even begins.

In preparing for Passover, housewives often tried to re-create the foods of this holiday—popovers, matzoh kugel, matzoh *brei*,* sponge cake, macaroons—that their mothers and grandmothers had taught them to make. At Passover time, Jewish women who had moved away from keeping traditional homes were more likely to purchase kosher meat and attend to the ritual niceties in readying the kitchen. Often this was done in deference to elderly observant *baubies* (grandmothers).

Although the holiday still entails a great deal of work today, there have been changes in outlook and styles of consumption. For example, many women eschew elaborate housecleaning, and the availability of a wide variety of ready-made Passover foods has made meal preparation easier. Indeed, the feast itself has stepped outside the home, for many synagogues now sponsor Seders.

Chanukah commemorates the 164 B.C.E. victory of a faction of Judeans, known as the Maccabees, over the oppressive Greco-Syrian king Antiochus IV Epiphanes, whose aim was to hellenize Judea. The holiday had a minor role in traditional Judaism. In America, however, Chanukah has assumed greater significance

---

*Kugel is an egg-rich pudding, generally made with noodles or potatoes. Matzoh *brei* is the Passover equivalent of French toast.

A cookbook produced by the Scopus chapter of Hadassah, Minneapolis, in 1975

because it falls in the period around Christmas, and it has been subject to the same commodification.

By the 1920s, assimilated mothers in the Upper Midwest began paying more attention to the holiday. Some created decorations and a more festive domestic atmosphere so that their children would not make invidious comparisons between Chanukah and Christmas. It was not until the post-World War II years, however, that home decoration became common, encouraged by synagogues that sponsored decorating contests. Tinsel and colored lights were added to the stock of synagogue gift shops. The Minneapolis Junior Chamber of Commerce, in an effort to be evenhanded, awarded prizes based on the most elaborate decorations to both Christian and Jewish homes during this period.

Women not only adorned their homes and created Chanukah parties, but they also replaced traditional menorahs (Chanukah candelabras) with ones made in Israel. Even the candles changed color, from the customary orange to multicolored and from United

In 1957 a shop display case at St. Paul's Temple of Aaron bore an assortment of Israeli-made ritual objects and giftware.

OPPOSITE PAGE:

Top left: Bessie Furman of Minneapolis had Chanukah decorations like this one made by a carpenter and an electrician in the early 1930s. She sold them to friends and used the proceeds to pay for her Hadassah pledge.

Top right: In the 1970s, Doris Kirschner made a gingerbread replica of her Minneapolis home as the centerpiece for her elaborate annual Chanukah cookie party. Note the menorah and dreidel in the front yard.

Bottom: Two members of the Minneapolis Junior Chamber of Commerce present Edith Linoff with a prize for her Chanukah decorations, 1953.

States-made to Israeli-manufactured. It was a way of supporting both the synagogue gift shop and the new state of Israel. Children now often receive elaborate gifts on each of the eight nights the holiday is celebrated rather than a small amount of spending money, as in the past. In culinary terms the celebration has changed as well. Latkes (potato pancakes) were the food most commonly associated with Chanukah.* Today, cookie cutters shaped like dreidels (tops) and menorahs subtly encourage parents to exchange, or at least add, baked goods to the latkes at a Chanukah party. The

*Customarily fried in olive oil, latkes symbolize the miracle that was said to have occurred when the Maccabees cleansed the Temple in Jerusalem following their victory. The scant amount of oil they found to relight the candelabra in the sanctuary—said to be enough to last only one day—burned for eight days.

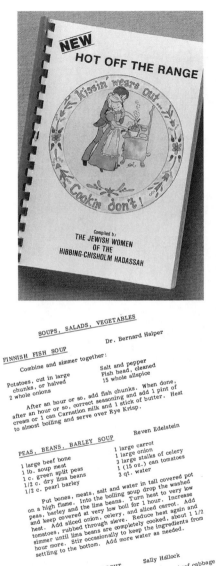

SOUPS, SALADS, VEGETABLES

Dr. Bernard Halper

FINNISH FISH SOUP

Combine and simmer together:

Potatoes, cut in large
chunks, or halved
2 whole onions

Salt and pepper
Fish head, cleaned
15 whole allspice

After an hour or so, add fish chunks. When done,
after an hour or so, correct seasoning and add 1 pint of
cream or 1 can Carnation milk and 1 stick of butter. Heat
to almost boiling and serve over Rye Krisp.

PEAS, BEANS, BARLEY SOUP

Reven Edelstein

1 large beef bone
1 lb. soup meat
1 c. green split peas
1/2 c. dry lima beans
1/2 c. pearl barley

1 large carrot
1 large onion
3 large stalks of celery
1 (15 oz.) can tomatoes
3 qt. water

Put bones, meats, salt and water in tall covered pot
on a high flame. Into the boiling soup drop the washed
peas, barley and the lima beans. Turn heat to very low
and keep covered at very low boil for 1 hour. Increase
heat. Add sliced onion, celery, and sliced carrot. Add
tomatoes, rubbed through sieve. Reduce heat again and
simmer until lima beans are completely cooked, about 1 1/2
hour more. Stir occasionally to keep the ingredients from
settling to the bottom. Add more water as needed.

Sally Hallock

INSTANT MEAT BORSCHT

1 jar beet borscht

2 cans kosher beef cabbage
soup

Heat together; simmer for about 5 minutes. Tastes
just like your grandma made.

A Hadassah cookbook produced in 1981 on Minnesota's Iron Range

holiday is malleable, and women are actively molding it to fit their families' needs.

•

Along with changes in the celebration of holidays have come changes in cuisine. Immigrant Jewish women began sharing recipes with non-Jewish neighbors as soon as both parties could arrive at a common language. Sarah Thal in North Dakota and other late-nineteenth-century Upper Midwestern Jewish farm wives learned from American neighbors how to prepare the pancakes, pies, and pot roasts that were expected by the visiting threshing crews. The neighbors, in turn, learned Thal's German recipes for kuchen.

This exchange was intra-ethnic as well. For example, recipe swaps between Lithuanian and Rumanian immigrants helped forge a hybrid Jewish-American cuisine. The culinary differences between the former, who used schmaltz (rendered poultry fat) as the fat of choice and the latter, who used oil, grew insignificant. Local ingredients, too, had an effect. Housewives learned to prize Lake Superior trout for flavoring gefilte fish; in the Old Country, the staple fish had been carp. "Pike and whitefish and a little bit of trout. I didn't like buffalo [fish]," declared Dorothy Mosow Hurwitz of Sioux Falls, South Dakota, in 1995 when describing her recipe. But there were continuities as well. Rose Rapaport Schwartz, who grew up on a farm near Wishek, North Dakota, remembered a neighboring farm with a cherry orchard: "[A]nd when the cherries were ripe all the friends of my mother's would come, prick them with hairpins and make jams and wishnik [an Eastern European cordial]."

Commercial food producers also informed immigrant housewives about new products and recipes, for their Jewish target market was both literate and receptive to change. Yiddish-English cookbooks published in the 1920s and 1930s by Twin Cities-based flour companies such as Gold Medal and Pillsbury helped standardize Jewish-American cooking, while introducing Jewish women to American foods such as baking powder biscuits and shortcake.

The second and third generations of Jewish women, fully comfortable in English, published dozens of cookbooks of their own as fund-raisers for their synagogues and favorite philanthropic organizations. These books now serve as windows on the culinary fashions of the decades in which they were produced. But many also indicate the ethnic influence of neighbors as well as of locally and regionally available foods. For example, *Hot off the Range,* the cookbook published by the Hibbing-Chisholm chapter of Hadassah in 1981 has recipes for Finnish, Italian, Cornish, and Slovenian dishes. (Hibbing and Chisholm are located on the Mesabi Iron Range.) This cookbook also contains numerous recipes employing blueberries, which grow abundantly in the north woods.

The newer cookbooks chart still other changes in Jewish life. The segregation in them of traditional Jewish cuisine into "holiday" or "traditional" sections speaks volumes about how segmented modern Jewish life has become. The "traditional" Eastern European recipes are generally used only for major yearly holidays such as Passover and Rosh Hashanah, or, less frequently, for the Sabbath. The reasons for this change are numerous. Few modern American women have time for the hours-long simmering and braising of casseroles or the rolling, filling, and crimping of individual morsels. Furthermore, a cuisine based on potatoes, rye bread, chicken fat, beans, cabbage, and inexpensive cuts of meat—all designed to supply calories cheaply to poor people—finds few takers among today's health-conscious and more affluent Jews. Starting in the 1960s, Israeli recipes, Middle Eastern and Mediterranean in origin, began to be included in the cookbooks produced by synagogues and women's organizations. In one sense, this development reflects a movement toward a healthier cuisine. In a deeper sense, though, the inclusion of such recipes is yet another indicator of how American Jews have identified with Israelis. In fact, it can be seen as a sort of "kitchen Zionism."

·

Despite the deconsecration of the kitchen with the decline of kashrut observance, despite the sometimes radical innovations in holiday celebration, and despite the fitting of erstwhile daily Jewish food into a "holiday" niche, there remain numerous domestic tasks that tie the Jewish woman to her religion. A woman's presence and persistence—indeed, her willingness to plan, prepare, and shop—are still necessary if holidays are to be observed. At the holiday table, prayers are said, recipes are passed on, families are reunited, and children are indoctrinated.

But who is to serve as domestic-ritual director and cook as more and more Jewish mothers move toward full-time employment? A great many working women feel they do not have the time to prepare for holidays or run traditional households in the manner of their mothers. And they do not wish to be reproached about this. At present, Jewish communities all over the nation are becoming aware that they must work together to devise new ways for Jewish families to celebrate their holidays and, indeed, take pleasure in all aspects of being Jewish.

VOICES

KEEPING KOSHER: TOWN AND COUNTRY

In the early 1880s Sarah Thal and her husband were pioneers in what became Nelson County, North Dakota.

A newcomer must of course experience much embarrassment. My worst was one day [when] Mr. Mendelson brought in a crate of pork and asked me, a piously reared Jewess, to cook it. In time I consented. However, I never forgot my religious teachings. I did, however, discard the dietary laws and practices, but to this day I observe the Passover (New Year's Day) and the Yon Kipper [*sic*].

———

Beginning in 1905, Joe Dokovna's parents farmed near Wing, North Dakota, an area where a number of Jewish farmers lived.

We were too far from a kosher butcher shop, we never had pork or milk and meat together at the table. We tried to keep as kosher as we could. . . . Whenever a rabbi came through they would have him slaughter chickens, or they would slaughter a cow or something, then they divided the meat. That was the only kosher meat they would have until the railroad was built through Regan and Wing. Then they could ship in kosher meat from the Twin Cities.

———

In 1910 Frieda Aurach Marcowitz's family homesteaded near Ashley, North Dakota.

When we first came . . . there was no Jewish meat to be bought. So for two years my mother didn't taste a piece of meat, and then she was losing her sight. She went to a doctor, and he said that she would either have to get her kind of meat or start eating the *goyish* [non-Jewish] meat, otherwise she would get blind.

———

The fourteen-member Halpern family, living in Hebron, North Dakota, in the 1910s, fared no better, as daughter Blanche Halpern Goldberg recalled. The all-purpose rabbi she remembered came from Minneapolis.

When any Jewish baby was born, . . . my father would contact [Rabbi Heiman] to come out and circumcise the [boys]. . . . So when he did come out to do that, he would kill chickens and geese and everything for my mother, and they smoked it to have kosher meat. We imported kosher meat from Minneapolis, but when it came out by train, and our store was across the street from the station, the stationmaster said [to my father], "Jake, your package came." He said, "I know, Pete. Dump it. It smells way over here already." No refrigeration. How my mother managed to feed all those kids with very little meat, I still don't know.

———

Ida Cohen Golberg's family farmed on the outskirts of Duluth during the first two decades of this century.

Although we lived in the country we kept a very strict kosher house. We would come to the city as my Dad would go down every day to deliver milk. My mother would make her own bread and butter and cheese, but the meat we would buy in a butcher shop. There were three or four kosher butcher shops in Duluth.

––––––

Jewish women gave up their culinary customs slowly and reluctantly. Gladys Jacobs Field's grandparents were German Jews who settled in Minneapolis in 1873. They had seven children.

Well, my grandmother's idea of keeping kosher was not what anybody else would consider keeping kosher. . . . [B]ut she was very firm about what she believed in doing. . . . [T]hey didn't wash the dishes together. . . . You know, separate dishes. . . . And they didn't . . . eat any pork. And they did fast on the holidays. My mother was the only one of her generation who did all these things.

––––––

Florence Shuman Sher's family lived in West Union, Iowa, during the first several decades of this century.

[My father] gradually wore down my Mother's wish to have nothing but kosher meat in our home. (This was long before the time of refrigerated freight cars and when the kosher meat, shipped from Dubuque, reached West Union in the summer it was fit for neither man nor beast!)

Gradually then, my Mother's inbred beliefs were put aside but my Mother never set foot inside a "trayfe" (unkosher) meat market. She always insisted that my father do this shopping (perhaps as a sly punishment). But even though the meat came to her un-

kosher, she still used to salt and soak the meat . . . in the orthodox way she had been trained to do, and thus she lived up to her
religious beliefs as best she could.

———

*Cecyle Eirinberg Marsh's family lived in a succession of small
South Dakota towns during the 1920s.*

My mother kept kosher in all these little towns. We had train
service—you know how train service was in those days. She
would order meat out of Sioux City and it would come spoiled.
She would throw it out, so we lived on milchig for most of the
time, salmon and cheese. . . . It was a big problem for her. When I
got married she said, "Daughter, I couldn't change, but I don't
want you to keep kosher." She knew I was going to live in a small
town. She told me not to.

———

*Bernice Banen of Hibbing recalled how the interurban street-
car, which connected Chisholm and Hibbing before World War I,
helped women prepare for the Sabbath.*

Every home [in Hibbing] kept kosher. . . . [But] the [shochet]
was in Chisholm five miles away. . . . Well they just got on the
streetcar with the chicken and put them in . . . an orange crate.
. . . They would go to Chisholm and get them killed and brought
them back to Hibbing and sometimes one woman would take
many chickens to . . . other people.

———

*Anne Garon Greenberg and her husband, Charles, lived in
St. Paul. He died in 1961.*

I always got kosher meats as long as my husband was alive. . . .
Let's put it that way. I started kosher with four sets of dishes—no,
five. One for Passover, glass dishes for Passover . . . and the other

was a good set for fleishig and an everyday set.* [Then] a good set for milchig and an everyday one. And gradually they merged. I don't know what happened, but they all merged. . . . And the same with the silver.

———

Anne Rothenberg Zabel's mother tried an easy system for keeping order in her 1920s Sioux City, Iowa, kitchen.

Now all my mother's milchig dishtowels had blue embroidery on them and all the fleishig dishtowels had red embroidery on them, so you had no excuse for mixing them up. . . . But once in a while they would mix them up anyway, and she would have a fit.

After her marriage and move to Sioux Falls, South Dakota, Zabel kept kosher only when her mother lived with her.

I never felt that keeping kosher was a must. Although if you look at it as a disciplinary action it would be very effective, but I didn't feel I needed it because I spent lots and lots of time and energy and money on Jewish things.

———

Cecilia Rose Waldman's mother arrived in St. Paul at the turn of the century and married in 1917. After Waldman's father died in 1956, her mother came to live with her. Together they negotiated an intermediary position, one that relied more on practicality than Jewish law.

My mother always kept a kosher home, her mother before her kept a kosher home, she didn't know anything but kashrut. But when she came to live with us we had a problem. I, too, started

———

*Glass dishes, unlike pottery or china, are considered nonporous. With proper boiling, they can be used for Passover.

out with keeping a kosher home. In World War II things were hard to come by. My husband said his mother was only eating hardboiled eggs and herring in our house anyway. [He said,] "Let's forget the whole thing about kashrut," and so I mixed my dishes and I didn't keep kosher.

So when my mother came to live with me . . . I said, "How are we going to manage? My husband doesn't want it, my children don't know from it. My dishes are mixed." I'll never forget her answer for a woman of her generation. She said, "Cec, I eat in restaurants. I really don't care about your pots and your pans or your silverware, but I would choke to death if I had to eat non-kosher meat." So I said, "There is no problem. Whenever we sit down as a family I'll buy kosher meat, and you cook it." So that was how we lived for over twenty years.

RECENT EFFORTS TO KEEP KOSHER

Dr. James M. Strosberg wrote to Beatrice Premack of Aberdeen, South Dakota, in October 1987 in response to a request she had made to past members of B'nai Isaac synagogue to help her in preparing a history of Jewish life in that city.

[W]e were stationed at Eagle Butte[,] South Dakota at the Public Health Service Indian Hospital from 1968 to 1970. . . . We had just been married for 2 years . . . and you were so kind to arrange kosher meat for us. I imagine your mother picked it up in Omaha and it was flown to Aberdeen and then a laundry man named Elmer drove it down from Aberdeen to Eagle Butte when he made his dry cleaning run. I guess our kosher meat traveled the furthest of any other Jew in the United States, around 800 miles!

———

In the present day some Jewish women, such as Carol Porter Berlin, who in the 1980s lived in St. Paul, begin keeping kosher when they get married or start having children. They find that kashrut offers a way to introduce spirituality into everyday life.

My mother in Minot . . . did not keep kosher. After Steve and I married [in the 1980s], and when we had Rebecca we decided to keep kosher. . . . We had the rabbi come in. . . . He took all our pots and pans outside, and he torched them and they were glowing. He brought a blowtorch to burn off the residue of *treyf* cooking.

FRIDAY-NIGHT SABBATH RECOLLECTIONS

Ida Levitan Sanders worked at the Talmud Torah of Minneapolis in the 1920s. The school was then located in a densely Jewish neighborhood on the city's North Side, which encompassed Orthodox and Conservative synagogues and well-to-do and struggling Jews alike.

I remember Dr. [George] Gordon, who later became director at the Talmud Torah. [He] was taking me somewhere . . . and as we were going up and down the streets, we could literally smell the Sabbath, the fish and the chicken . . . [a]nd that was when he said that the "rey-ach" [aroma] was as important as the "ru-ach" [spirit].

———

Nellie Brody Werner grew up on a farm near Regan, North Dakota, that her father owned from 1898 to 1920.

Come Friday night all of us were ready to welcome the Sabbath. The candles were kindled. My Friday job was polishing the brass candle holders with ashes. My mother brought these candle holders from Russia, and I still use them. My father always recited the Kiddush. The wine was choke cherry wine that we had the year round. My mother made delicious choke cherry wine.

———

Sylvia Kremen Rosenberg's family farmed near Wilton, North Dakota, roughly between 1900 and 1920.

Ida Geller of Fargo, North Dakota,
placing Sabbath candles, about
1950

Picture in your mind a Friday. It is Erev Shabbos [the time before sundown, when the Sabbath commences]. The kitchen is filled with the aroma of fresh baked bread, chicken soup, carrot *zimmis** [*sic*], gefilte fish, roast chicken and [the] enticing smell of fresh baked pie. The table is covered with a white linen cloth. The best dishes and silver adorn the table. At one end of the table is Father's Kiddish [*sic*] cup, the prayer book, the wine, and the Challah covered with a cloth of white. At the opposite end of the table stand Mother's silver candle sticks.

The men of the house have come in from the fields earlier than on [the] other days. The chores are completed. Everyone has cleaned up and put on fresh clothes. (Believe it or not, we took our baths in a wash tub.)

Now all is ready for the Sabbath prayer, and then the delicious food.

My Mother places a beautiful embroidered shawl over her head and lights the Sabbath candles, softly chanting the prayer.

Father fills the wine glasses for the older members around the table. (I remember my sister and I had "something" in our wine glasses. I don't think it was wine.) Father raises his Kiddish cup and recites the Kiddish prayer. Those of us, at the table, who know the prayer, sing along with him.

The Challah is cut. Each receiving a slice for the "Moitza" [prayer over bread].

The prayers are over. The food is served. Contentment and peace reign in the home. In the heart of each, there is love of God and thankfulness for all His blessings, and for the privilege of living in the Land of Freedom—America.

———

Hyman Greenstein recalled turn-of-the-century Sabbath preparations on his family's farm, which was located on the outskirts of North Minneapolis.

Sophie Frishberg slicing a challah at the St. Paul Jewish Community Center, about 1965

*Carrots that are first cooked and then browned in fat and sugar so that they glisten and taste sweet. Recipes for tzimmes and gefilte fish date back to medieval times. Both are eaten on the Sabbath in the hope that a prosperous week will follow.

[E]very day was bake day and especially Fridays when the challa was baked for the Sabbath. Oh they were really beautiful. Mother had a way of braiding bread with eight braids which is unusual in itself and then she would gloss over the top of the bread with the yellow of egg and when the bread was baked it would come out shiny and golden.

———

Marion Newman's parents bought a furniture store in Brainerd, Minnesota, in 1922 and lived there for several decades. The 1920s were years characterized by rising anti-Semitism.

On Friday night you'd light the candles as we did in our home, but somehow they were placed in a position where maybe a passerby wouldn't notice them. . . . We didn't want to call attention to the rite. . . . It tells of the insecurity that existed in those years in Brainerd.

———

Daniel J. Elazar recalled his aunt Rose Barzon Goldman telling him how life in Minneapolis about 1910 changed her family's religious customs.

You know my parents . . . had to keep their grocery store open on Shabbas [Sabbath]. . . . So Friday nights, we would retreat into the back room, light the candles as if Shabbas had come for all of us, and then my father would go back to tend the store.

PASSOVER RECOLLECTIONS

Sophie Turnoy Trupin described, among other things, how everyday utensils could be prepared for Passover use. Her family lived on a farm near Wilton, North Dakota, in the 1910s.

Several days before Passover, . . . my mother, sister, and I set about getting our home ready for the holiday. Mother whitewashed all the walls and scoured the floors. She made the utensils kosher for Passover with scalding hot water. A stone was first heated in the range until it was red hot. It was then put into a very large pot of boiling water, making the water sizzle and hiss. The utensils were boiled for some time in this water. In addition, every piece of furniture was carried down to the [slough] and scrubbed and allowed to dry on the bank where the young grass was just beginning to appear.

———

Anne Rothenberg Zabel's devout family lived in Sioux City, Iowa, in the early part of the century.

When we got ready for Passover we even washed the door-knobs. We had a . . . library with books in many languages. *Erev Pesach** my mother would make me go through every one of those books, shake them out, God forbid someone would be reading a book and a crumb would fall out. I was fifteen years old before I saw the end of a Seder because I was so dead tired by the time the first Seder came along.

———

Nellie Brody Werner's recollection of a winter about 1910 is another reminder of how nature affected all aspects of life on the Dakota prairies.

One winter we were snowbound for so long, my mother baked our own matzos. The trains weren't running and our Passover order was delayed somewhere.

———

By the 1930s, Marion Newman's mother had stopped keeping kosher because of the unreliability of kosher meat sent from Duluth to her home in Brainerd.

---

*Literally, Passover before sundown. (Jewish holidays begin at sundown.) In this case it would refer to the afternoon before the holiday began, when the last housecleaning details were attended to.

We did not keep Kosher. Except for one week, the week of Passover. Every dish in our home was out. My mother . . . bought food from Minneapolis. Any rabbi in America could eat in our home for one week a year. . . . The rest of the year there was one set of dishes in the house and in the early years we didn't serve butter with meat but in due course we got over that and butter was served with meat, milk and so on.

———

Dorothy Mosow Hurwitz lived in Sioux Falls, South Dakota. Her grandmother came from Sioux City, Iowa, to visit for the holiday up through the 1940s.

The only time I kept strictly kosher was the week of Passover, because Grandma Kruger would come. We ordered meat from Minneapolis and fish from Duluth. We used all grandma's pots. We had an old bake box that came from the Old Country, and in there were the *pesadicka* [Passover] dishes and the silver and the pots and the pans. . . . There weren't three dishes alike.

———

Rose Levy Overbach, who lived in St. Cloud, Minnesota, during the 1920s, recalled that Jewish strangers were not forgotten either.

The Jewish families used to get together and make a *Pesach* dinner and take it out to Jewish boys in the State Reformatory that were prisoners.

———

Laura Rapaport Borsten's parents first farmed in McIntosh County, North Dakota, in the first decade of this century and moved to nearby Wishek about five years later. Her mother had been a seamstress in Europe.

Mother made all clothing for the girls. The eldest got new clothes, the rest hand-me-downs. I got a new dress for *Pesach* and a new dress for Rosh Hashanah. Don't forget, everything came off one bolt. . . . [E]verything in the house was the same.

EVERYDAY FOOD, JEWISH FOOD, AND THE CREATION OF A JEWISH-AMERICAN CUISINE

In the early 1900s Elizabeth Banick Sherman's family lived in Grand Forks, North Dakota, where her father was a peddler and her mother kept a cow for the family's dairy needs.

Hitched onto the back of our home was . . . the summer kitchen. . . . All around that room hung frozen geese, ducks, chickens and beef. We kids used to be scared to go in there. . . . [There were] great big barrels of frozen apples, frozen sour tomatoes, . . . sauerkraut, and always 2 big barrels of frozen sour pickles. . . . Oh how we little ones disliked going into the summer kitchen in 30 below weather. First we would remove the lids from the barrel, then the cloth covering, then a big slimy rock, then another slimy wooden cover, then we were at the sour pickles. We'd fill a pot with them to take [to] the house, and then we had to wash off the rock and boards and recover the whole barrel as we had found it. Our hands would be red and frozen, but were those pickles ever good! . . .

I must write about our cellar. Many cellars in those early 1900 years were like ours. You got into the cellar by lifting up a door in the kitchen under the kitchen table. Then, you walked down a few stairs, and the dampness and smells hit you right away. There were shelves all around the cellar (more of my mother's hard work) with jars of home made peaches, apples, pears, plums, cherries, and as those were prohibition days, there were jars or bottles of cherry vishnik, blackberry vishnik and other vishniks [cordials] that I can't remember.

In the 4 corners of the cellar (earth floors, no cement) were piles of sand mixed with sawdust, I think, in mound forms. In each of these mounds were buried carrots, cabbages, onions, potatoes, beets and every kind of vegetable that would keep well for the whole winter. Also on some shelves stood big white jars of our cow's milk being made into sour cream, cheese . . . (sweet cream) butter. . . . We were handed the jar and told to sit and shake it until it turned into delicious sweet butter. Three times a week our hands nearly fell off making butter.

Sherman's recollections also show how, in the Upper Midwest, a hallmark recipe of Jewish cuisine accommodated regional fish.

Every Thursday in those early years of the 1900's, my father would receive a big box of fish from Warroad, Minnesota. The Jews of Grand Forks came and picked out the fish they had ordered. My father weighed them, and carp, I remember, was 8 cents a pound, buffalo was 8 cents a pound, some fish called gold eyes sold for 25 cents a fish. There couldn't have been much profit in it for my father. Every Friday we smelled the "gifilte fish" cooking.

————

Laura Rapaport Borsten's description of food consumed on her family's farm and in the Jewish triangle bounded by the towns of Lehr, Ashley, and Wishek, North Dakota, indicates the amount of recipe-trading that went on in the late 1910s and 1920s.

We ate egg noodles, cottage cheese and vegetables, bread [baked] twice a week—rye bread and challah. We woke up Friday to the smell of Bialys. They were flat [rolls] and had onion in the middle and poppyseed. We ate beef stew and leftover bread with lots of garlic—we could not go back to school after that. . . . We had a mixture there of the foods of the Rumanians, which means eggplant, strudel, *mamaliga* [cornmeal mush] and could mean pompotchkas [meatballs]. . . . You had the mixture of the *Litfaks* [Lithuanians], which my mother was. That was chopped herring. I know she was famous for the chopped liver and the chopped herring—no one [else] made it so well.

————

Morris Freedland's family, who farmed near Osseo, Minnesota, in the 1910s, were socialists. But socialists, too, ate what was familiar to them.

Although our family didn't observe religious customs, they did retain many of the cultural features of Judaism. For example, they ate only kosher food. . . . [My mother] was an excellent cook, and in addition to some of the vegetable dishes like borsht and sweet corn fresh from the field, she always served herring. Herring was a staple of the diet back in Dvinsk [in Latvia], but it could also be a delicacy. Ma . . . prepared herring . . . in three ways: it could be served raw and sliced plus raw onion, or it could be served chopped up with stale bread as a paste or pate. The ultimate way for a more festive occasion was to bake it on the red hot coals of the stove until the skin turned black.

———

By the 1930s, the Rapaport family had moved from Wishek to Minneapolis. Laura, who had by then earned a bachelor's degree in library science, organized the Adath Jeshurun synagogue library. As she recalled, Albert Gordon, the congregation's rabbi, recommended her to the Sarasota Flour Company as a translator.

[The flour company] had done a contest about why people use Sarasota Flour, and they made the mistake of putting the information about the contest in the Jewish papers in Chicago, and they got fifty entries at least. Minnesota was pretty strict about contests. . . . So they asked if I could translate these Yiddish entries they got because they had to consider them. . . . The Jewish contestants used the opportunity to tell how they came to America, and how they had suffered[,] . . . a regular *bintel brief* [the melodramatic letters to the editor of the New York-based Jewish daily newspaper, *The Forward*].

They recommended me to the Pillsbury Flour Company [which] wanted to do a cookbook. So my job was to go around and help them pick out recipes for things that used lots of flour—

Pillsbury's Yiddish-English cook-booklet, mid-1930s, translated by Laura Rapaport Borsten

like blintzes [and] knishes . . . and then to get the recipe from these people.*

And I don't know about your mother, but my mother would [say] "*shit arein* [pour it in], put in, feel it, until it's right." . . . I asked . . . everyone I knew, my mother, my aunt Rose, my aunt Lena, the lady who lived downstairs. . . . Anyhow [the company] would take it back to their kitchen and establish proper recipes.

*Pillsbury published the four-page booklet in the mid-1930s.

. . . Then they gave it back to me . . . to be translated into proper Yiddish.

———

The May 1925 minutes of the Fargo, North Dakota, Hebrew Ladies Aid Society indicate how Mazola corn oil established itself as a kitchen staple. It was particularly welcome in Jewish kitchens because it did not become rancid as quickly as schmaltz did.

[It was decided that] the Ladies Society should give a picnic. . . . A committee was appointed. Sister Sophie Naftalin, Sarah Rivkin and Pres. E Wiengarten to serve doughnuts and same are supposed to be made in the mazo [sic] oil, so to demonstrate to the ladies how good that oil is. It was moved that all the ladies from the society are asked to order their oil when needed through the agency Mr Wm. Gilles or Zimmerman's grocery. So .60 from every gallon purchased goes toward the Ladies Aid Society.

CHAPTER FOUR

"We Dug More Rocks"
Women and Work

It was a tremendous transition for mother. She was a very fine seamstress and had worked in Bialystock making shirts for the army. . . . Here she was out in the bleak North Dakota prairie, living in a shack, no running water, no inside bathroom, cold in the winter, hot in the summer, and what they were doing was pulling the stones away so they could plow the land.

LAURA RAPAPORT BORSTEN'S mother's transition from an urban sewing room to the rough Upper Midwestern prairie in the early 1900s is typical of the adjustment many immigrant Jewish women made to the region's labor climate. She, like an estimated 70 percent of young Jewish females registered as artisans in the Pale of Settlement, had worked in the needle trades. Once transplanted to the Upper Midwest, though, they typically found themselves in settings, both rural and urban, where these skills were not in great demand. The economy and geography of the region dictated that Jewish women's work would diversify in ways few immigrants dreaming of America could have imagined.

Employment opportunities for these women contrasted sharply not only with the ones they had known in Europe but also with those prevailing in large American cities such as New York and Chicago, where the burgeoning ready-made clothing industry employed vast numbers of Jewish immigrants. But in the cities of the Upper Midwest, that industry was small and centered in shops that typically employed fewer than a half-dozen people each.

The economic well-being of the Upper Midwest was founded on agriculture, mining, grain milling, and forestry. Few Jews ever worked in the latter three areas. However, they experimented with farming, and they filled a traditional niche by providing commercial services to miners, millers, lumberjacks, and farmers. Farming, for a brief period, provided Jewish immigrants with what was long considered the quintessential American work experience—that of the independent yeoman farmer. With greater or lesser enthusiasm, Jewish women learned to be farm wives. And, as spouses of

Main Street merchants all over the Upper Midwest, they balanced their Old World role as contributors to the family economy with the New World middle-class expectation that wives should be removed from the hurly-burly of the business world.

Daughters of Jewish immigrants commonly pursued white-collar jobs as bookkeepers and clerks, positions in which regional particularities did not figure. Those who could afford additional schooling characteristically chose teaching. Unlike East Coast Jewish women, who typically taught in large urban areas, many Upper Midwestern women who entered this field performed stints in small-town or rural settings.

•

The notion of farming as a livelihood was both politically improbable and emotionally alluring to Jews in czarist Russia. The czarist regimes would not allow Jews to own land, but the populist cultural nationalism of the times held that a life on the land was worthier than one spent in commercial ventures. Impelled by this ideology, Jews on three continents commenced farming in the late 1800s. By the early 1900s Zionists had established kibbutzim (collective farms) in Palestine, Jewish gauchos were riding the pampas in Argentina, and Jews were farming and ranching on the Dakota plains of the United States.

During the greater part of the massive Eastern European Jewish immigration to America that took place between 1880 and 1924, homestead land was plentiful in the Dakotas. As noted earlier, homesteading was an affordable option for those with little money and plenty of hope and fortitude. The first Jewish farming colonies in the region, founded in the early 1880s, were Painted Woods and Devils Lake in present-day North Dakota and Bethlehem Yehudah and Cremieux in what is now South Dakota. They were all short lived, lasting on average less than five years. However, the news of free land printed in the Yiddish press in Russia and the eastern United States, combined with letters from friends, continued to draw Jewish would-be farmers to the plains. After the colonies had failed, Jews generally farmed in informal clusters, from roughly 1895 to 1910. The isolated Jewish farm was a rarity.

Many Jewish farmers received help in the form of loans from congregations. Rabbi Judah Wechsler, who led the Mount Zion Hebrew Congregation in St. Paul, was an ardent advocate of the Painted Woods colony, while the Devils Lake colonists were first aided by congregants of Minneapolis's Shaari Tof (Temple Israel). Sustained aid came from philanthropic societies such as the Jewish Agriculturalists Aid Society and the Jewish Agricultural Society, based in Chicago and New York City, respectively. Both organizations provided loans for land purchase and start-up capital and sent out representatives to determine results. According to figures collected by sociologist J. Sanford Rikoon, 460 farmers in Minnesota and the Dakotas took out loans between 1888 and 1933. Beginning in 1908, the New York society also published a Yiddish-English magazine, *The Jewish Farmer,* which offered technical and agricultural advice.

The number of Jews who took out homestead deeds in the period from 1880 to 1910 is hard to pin down. Sociologist William Sherman estimated that, in those years, at least eight hundred Jews filed for deeds in North Dakota. Among these, several dozen were women—widows and other unmarried females.

The wives of these undercapitalized novice farmers often worked alongside their husbands to prepare the land and harvest the crops. "She worked in the fields digging rocks, pulling mustard, hauling hay, and shocking grain," recalled Samuel Dolf of his mother, Cecelia, who toiled on their Morton County, North Dakota, farm in 1903. The dust and heat at harvest time added to women's exhaustion. They also had children to contend with, "one child on the way, one cradled in her free arm, and another holding on to her skirt," recalled Craney Goldman Bellin, whose parents broke the sod in McKenzie County, North Dakota, around 1906.

When farmers could afford men to help out, women traded field work for that of feeding the harvest crews. In order to satisfy them, Jewish women learned to prepare American foods. Many, like Sarah Thal, who immigrated from Germany to what is now North Dakota in the early 1880s, kept gardens, preserved fruits and vegetables, made cottage cheese and butter, gathered eggs, and sewed for the whole family. Women also worked in groups. Rose Rapaport

Schwartz, for example, remembered her mother joining other Jewish farm women to pick and prepare rose petals and cherries for jams and cordials near their Ashley, North Dakota, farm in the early 1900s. The work went more quickly as they reminisced about life in the Old Country, exchanged recipes, worried about this year's crops, and shared hopes for the future. While Jewish farm women contributed to the family coffers through their domestic production, they helped in still other ways, selling butter and eggs in town and contracting to provide meals for local road crews.

These farm wives were not the only Jewish women milking cows and raising chickens. They were joined by women living in small towns and even in cities. St. Paul, where one Jewish-immigrant neighborhood was situated on a sparsely developed flood plain of the Mississippi, was a prime example. There, cows grazed and chickens scratched until after World War II. Edith Milavetz remembered her mother's work as an urban chicken farmer in St. Paul in the period around World War I. After the shochet killed the chickens, she recalled, the whole family would help pluck the feathers and deliver the birds to the buyers, using a child's wagon. The family also sold milk, butter, sour cream, and cottage cheese, and matzoh at Passover.

Farmers' daughters had numerous tasks as well. Tending the garden and helping with washing, ironing, and canning were customary chores. They did other work as the need or opportunity arose. For example, Lillian, Frieda, Jennie, and Nellie Brody drove their family's cows to pasture on their way to school, near Regan, North Dakota, in the 1910s. During the same period, young Sophie Turnoy, near Wilton, North Dakota, harvested wheat and received the same wages as men because, as her employer said, she "had . . . accomplished as much as any of the men."

The Jewish farming experience lasted from the early 1880s to about 1920. Although not long lived, the episode was an important one. For most Eastern European Jewish farmers, the very fact of owning land was a considerable accomplishment. They appreciated the personal freedom farming offered. Many families used their farms to establish an economic foothold, staying long enough to "prove them up" and sell them, which provided a resource for entry into another occupation. More often than not, such a move was necessary because farming on the arid plains was a risky enterprise. The homestead allotment of 160 acres was small, the climate was harsh, natural disasters were frequent, and crop prices were subject to violent fluctuations. In addition, Jewish parents with an eye to their children's education knew that rural schools ended at the eighth grade. Finally, they understood that the prospects of finding other Jews to marry in rural society were slim; the prospect of wedding a non-Jew was generally unacceptable. Farm unions like the weddings of Eva and Rose Kremenetsky to Joe and Charles Losk and Henry Kremenetsky to Dora Weinberg, all three of which occurred near Wilton, North Dakota, about 1910, were exceptions to the rule. By the 1920s, most Jewish farmers had moved to the

The Silberman general store, New Home, North Dakota, 1910

Hilda, Charles, and Zelda
Modelevsky in their St. Paul
grocery store, 1926

West Coast, to the Twin Cities, to regional centers such as Sioux
Falls or Minot, or to nearby small towns that served the farming
population. Nearly all who moved to towns opened stores.

Their establishments were of several varieties. Those on the
plains were general stores that sold clothing, boots, lanterns,
saddles, canned goods, blankets, and hundreds of other items
farmers and ranchers needed. The proprietors of such operations
generally were the only Jewish families in town. Other stores were
located in the larger railroad hubs, in mining and market towns, and
in the cities. In these places Eastern European Jews joined countrymen who had started as peddlers and become minor merchants
and scrap dealers and German Jews who were well-established merchants. Virtually all the stores sold clothing, although a few
specialized in meat or groceries.

Women worked in all these varied locales. Wives generally served
by acting as salesclerks, bookkeepers, or, less frequently, by actually running the stores. Their involvement was crucial to the success
of the family enterprise, although as "helpers" they are invisible
in the census, a prime source of statistical data for the period of

Ann Goldstein and her children Al and Esther next to the family general store in Solen, North Dakota, late 1930s

major immigration. (Censuses counted women as having no occupation unless they earned wages.) Even if their employment went unlisted, however, it is certain that many women worked in family-owned businesses. For example, a study of the roughly sixty Jewish families living in the Mesabi Iron Range town of Virginia between 1920 and 1940 indicated that about twenty of the wives worked, the majority in their husbands' stores. The many accounts and the numerous photos of husbands and wives behind the counters of their stores further attest to a joint effort.

There were many benefits to "helping out." Women could help earn a living for their families while not violating a long-held Jewish distaste for wives being supervised by other men. Helping out also gave married women a great deal of flexibility, for they could schedule their store hours around housework and child rearing. The utmost flexibility was achieved when the family lived behind or

Fannie Cohen's grocery store on
St. Paul's West Side, about 1915

above the store, as was common. Women who had clerked in city
stores or had done sales work prior to marriage often welcomed
such labor as a respite from minding children and keeping house.
Finally, helping out was a way to befriend the customers and offer
better service, particularly to farm wives. Jewish wives might note
the growth of customers' children, pull out the new bolts of fabric
attractive for clothing, and exchange recipes or household hints.
Store work also provided Jewish women with some measure of
social intercourse, sorely lacking for them in small towns domi-
nated by church activities.

Some women were freely recognized as partners. Emma Herbst
helped out as her husband established a large department store in
Fargo. After his death in 1910, she was "the guiding light" of the
store until her son became old enough to take control. Similarly,
Lena Oreckovsky and Fannie Goldfine were vital partners in their
husbands' businesses in Duluth. Oreckovsky worked in the family
department stores, named Oreck's, from the 1890s until 1927. Her
last title was president. Goldfine took care of bookkeeping and
financing and was a one-woman consumer-relations department

in the family's cattle-buying and feed businesses and furniture stores from the time of her marriage in the 1920s until the 1960s.

Other women had rather loose business partnerships with their husbands. Rose Levy Overbach's mother ran the family grocery store in St. Cloud, Minnesota, while her husband peddled fruit. In Lael Singer-Miller's family account, *Rachel* (1980), each evening during the early decades of the century, the mother, Rachel, cut cloth into five-yard pieces. These were sold to peddlers from the front room of her Duluth house. Her husband worked as a peddler.

Women also supplanted their spouses as heads of business, particularly if their husbands had difficulty learning English or were not able to make the transition from Talmudic study to American entrepreneurship. Other wives simply possessed a better business sense. Theodore Shuirman said that his mother "could add up four column numbers on sight" and was "the driving force" in the family's Keewatin, Minnesota, store, which opened in 1905, while his father "made up Yiddish stories for the kids."

Women also owned businesses in their own names. These ranged from peddling to large enterprises. For example, in the 1910 United States manuscript census, seven women on St. Paul's West Side were listed as storeowners. One had a secondhand store, two were

Mary T. Goldman was an entrepreneur who built a thriving business manufacturing hair products in St. Paul in the 1920s.

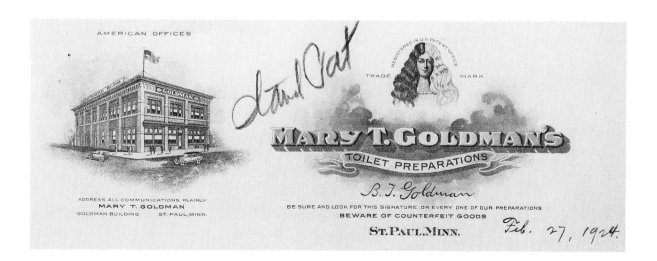

grocers, three had confectionery stores, and one was a peddler. All were listed as heads of households and so presumably were widows. Products aimed at the female market served as a niche for entrepreneurial women. Mary T. Goldman owned a large hair-products company bearing her name in St. Paul in the 1920s. Lena Kopelman created wigs and ran a beauty salon in Fargo in the early decades of the twentieth century. She also had a business agreement with the Fargo Hebrew Congregation to run the mikvah, which was located in the basement of her store (see p. 174).

Boarding was a form of helping out common in large cities; however, it was also practiced in smaller towns. It was a culturally acceptable economic activity, for it allowed married women to earn money without being supervised by strangers. The boarders and lodgers were often family members who had just arrived or landsleit (people from the same town or shtetl). One or two

AGES AT WHICH MARRIED JEWISH WOMEN TOOK IN BOARDERS

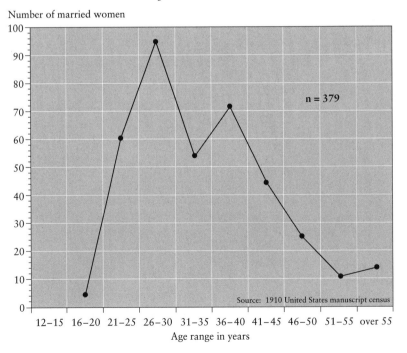

Number of married women

n = 379

Source: 1910 United States manuscript census

Age range in years

boarders was the average number per household. Jewish wives took in boarders when their children were young, generally stopped as children became teenagers, and resumed again, but to a lesser degree, later in life. One explanation for this pattern is that they only boarded when their children could not contribute to the family coffers, that is, when they were either too young or had moved out.

Twin Cities Jewish families may not have been so needy as those in New York City, however, for there were major differences between the numbers of those who took in boarders in the two locales. In 1910 the percentage of immigrant Jewish women in the Twin Cities who took in boarders was about half that of their counterparts in New York—27 percent versus 56 percent. There were differences as well between Italian and Jewish boarding patterns in St. Paul that reflected family need, demand, and potential for boarding and lodging. On St. Paul's West Side, the housing stock consisted of small houses and duplexes, whereas the Upper Town area, with its aging mansions, allowed Italian women to lodge great numbers of their compatriots who were employed as seasonal railroad laborers.

Table 1. WORK PROFILE OF JEWISH MOTHERS IN THREE TWIN CITIES IMMIGRANT NEIGHBORHOODS, 1910

Type of job	St. Paul West Side n=501 (%)	St. Paul Capitol City area n=210 (%)	Minneapolis North Side n=796 (%)
Boarding/lodging	26	33	22
All other [a]	3	5	3
No job [b]	71	62	75
Total	100	100	100

a. Storeowners, peddlers, dressmakers
b. The census listed only paid employment. Therefore, those working in family-run businesses were not counted.

Source: United States manuscript census, 1910

If mothers boarded and worked in family businesses, daughters, too, were expected to help. According to the 1910 United States manuscript census, the vast majority of Jewish girls in three Twin Cities immigrant neighborhoods—87 percent—stayed in school until age fifteen, although some worked after school. At age sixteen, roughly that same percentage went to work. While it may be shocking to learn that only 13 percent of Jewish girls were able to stay in high school, this percentage was twice as high as comparable figures gathered from East Coast cities and cited in the 1911 Immigration Commission report. The statistic is evidence that life was not quite so harsh for immigrant Jews in the Upper Midwest as in the East.

Upon leaving school, girls generally chose one of two paths, based on their educational plans, family financial resources, and acculturation. Those who had not been in America for long and who lacked English-language skills found factory work sewing garments, furs, or mattresses, making hats, or rolling cigars. The variety of factory jobs young Jewish women held reflects the fact that neither Minneapolis nor St. Paul was a garment-industry powerhouse like New York City.

Beginning in the 1860s, New York was the acknowledged center of the ready-made garment industry. By 1909, 40 percent of men's clothing in the country was manufactured there. Tens of thousands of women were employed making men's garments and, by the early twentieth century, even more labored in the burgeoning women's and children's clothing industry. Various sources centering on the year 1900 list between 40 and 77 percent of New York's Russian-Jewish females as garment workers.*

---

*Irving Howe, *World of Our Fathers* (New York: Harcourt Brace Jovanovich, 1976), 154, cites a "census" figure of 40 percent. Isaac M. Rubinow, "Economic and Industrial Condition: New York," in *The Russian Jew in the United States,* ed. Charles S. Bernheimer (1905; reprint, New York: Jerome S. Ozer, 1971), 112, writes that 77 percent of female Russian-Jewish workers were employed in the needle industries.

Table 2. WORK PROFILE OF JEWISH DAUGHTERS AGES SIXTEEN AND
OVER IN THREE TWIN CITIES IMMIGRANT NEIGHBORHOODS, 1910

Type of job	St. Paul West Side n=188 (%)	St. Paul Capitol City area n=117 (%)	Minneapolis North Side n=321 (%)
Factory/sewing	23	10	9
Factory/non-sewing	19	5	7
Small shop/sewing	15	18	11
Low white collar [a]	10	15	20
High white collar [b]	20	8	15
No job listed/in school	13	44	38
Total	100	100	100

a. Clerks, cashiers, messengers, wrappers
b. Department store saleswomen, bookkeepers, stenographers
Source: United States manuscript census, 1910

By contrast, in 1910, 23 percent of young Jewish women on
St. Paul's West Side sewed in the nineteen clothing factories then situated in that city. Only 9 percent worked as seamstresses in
Minneapolis's seven clothing factories. In 1910 fewer than a handful toiled at the Munsingwear Knitting Mills, which employed
about two thousand workers—this despite the fact that the factory was contiguous to the heavily Jewish North Side. Munsingwear's
very low number of Jewish workers may reflect anti-Semitism. But
it may also simply be an indication that, as was often the case, an
already-established ethnic group had made it a practice to secure all
available jobs for their own compatriots.*

Although the comparison made here is between New York
Jewish garment workers in 1900 and those in the Twin Cities in

---

*The factory's employee roster for 1920 contains a preponderance of Scandi-
navian and Finnish names. This is a reflection of Minneapolis's large Scandinavian population and of the fact that the city's main Finnish neighborhood
abutted the factory. Fewer than five Jewish names are on the roster.

1910, the differences are important. In 1910 New York's immigrant Jewish women were predominantly employed in garment factories whose payrolls included anywhere from twenty to more than one thousand workers. In the Twin Cities, significant numbers of Jewish women found needlework employment but in far smaller establishments. Eleven percent of the North Side's young immigrant Jewish women and 15 percent of St. Paul's worked in small tailoring shops, each of which had fewer than a half-dozen employees.

It is probably because so many Twin Cities Jewish women labored in small shops that union activity among them was muted. Few appear to have been involved in Local Number 171 of the United Garment Workers of America, established in the Twin Cities around 1909. Ten years later, when the first Twin Cities local of the Amalgamated Clothing Workers Union (ACWU) was established, its ranks included a fair number of Jewish women. However, the 1920

Simon Schwartz's tailor shop, St. Paul, 1917. Simon holds a measuring tape, and his wife, Sadie, is at the sewing machine.

A regional conference of the Workmen's Circle, St. Paul, 1918. Many Jewish women belonged to socialist organizations such as this one.

roll of union members striking Guiterman Brothers, a St. Paul clothing factory, lists only 9 of 258 female strikers who can be identified as Jewish. This is one sign that, by the time the unions were a strong force locally, young immigrant Jewish women had begun moving into white-collar work. Further evidence of the low level of union activity by this contingent comes from several other sources. In his 1949 study of Minneapolis Jewry from its beginnings to the 1930s, Rabbi Albert I. Gordon found only fifty Jewish women who were members of the ACWU in the 1930s. Finally, no Jewish women appear to have been involved in the bitter 1936 strike at Minneapolis's Strutwear Knitting Company.

The contrast between employment patterns among young immigrant Jewish women—who were well represented in the needle trades and almost absent from domestic service—and jobs held, for example, by Scandinavian women is striking. In 1910 less than 1 percent of Twin Cities immigrant Jewish women worked as domestics. By contrast, almost 63 percent of immigrant Swedish women were domestics during the same period. They found independence, good pay, and generally satisfactory working conditions in domestic service and greatly preferred it to the grueling farm labor they had left behind.

By about 1910, white-collar jobs began to be available to Jewish

The office of Berman Brothers Hides and Furs, Minneapolis, about 1910. Left to right: David and Fanny Berman, Jean Cohen.

Belle Zimmerman with her grade school class in a small Wisconsin town, about 1909

women who could speak English. The critical factor was not American birth but American education. Three or four years of schooling equipped young women for after-school work as cash girls and wrapping clerks. In 1910, 15 percent of Twin Cities immigrant Jewish daughters were employed in low white-collar work. Almost the same number, 14.3 percent, became saleswomen in department stores or trained to become stenographers or bookkeepers—then considered the acme of white-collar work. They generally gained such employment after attending business school, although some learned on the job. These figures correspond to national trends of the time.

The 1910 United States manuscript census provides a clear glimpse into the work patterns of a cohort of largely foreign-born mothers and daughters then living in the Twin Cities. The evidence available for the 1910s through the 1930s is sketchier, although the outlines are clear. Young unmarried women continued to seek white-collar work. As the general level of affluence among Jews rose, however, families began sending daughters to normal school or college. Daughters who worked in small-town family stores followed this pattern as well—as they did the unconcealed dictate that they were to find Jewish husbands. Some came back home and married storeowners, following in their mothers' footsteps. Others returned to their hometowns to teach. A multiyear teaching stint in a small town was commonplace. "It was a good experience," pronounced Sara Bashefkin Ryder of St. Paul about her sojourn in Nemadji, Minnesota, in 1929. "I wouldn't sell it for a million dollars and I wouldn't wish to repeat it for a million dollars." Social work was another common career. A list of graduates of the University of Minnesota School of Social Work from 1931 to 1993 contains roughly 140 Jewish women, or 7 percent of the graduates—more than twice as high as their percentage in the general population.

Diplomas, however, were no guarantee of jobs. Anti-Semitism between the end of World War I and World War II dashed the hopes of many young Jewish women. A report in a 1922 issue of the Twin Cities newspaper *American Jewish World* pointed to the fact that

there were no Jewish teachers in any Minneapolis high schools.*
Blanche Halpern Goldberg recalled that a mentor at the University of Minnesota in the late 1920s urged her to have her photographs, which would be shown to school superintendents who were hiring teachers, reshot. "She said to me," Blanche related, 'You ought to take them over again so you don't look so Jewish. Your hair is too curly.'"

The Depression made a bad situation worse. By 1931 an employment service was formed in Minneapolis to help Jewish women and men find work. While it was somewhat effective, the service could not address the root assumptions that led to prejudicial hiring. As late as 1939, the head of the division of dental hygiene at the University of Minnesota informed three Jewish students that they had less chance of being hired than gentiles. The underlying assumption that Jewish women had to endure such job discrimination became increasingly intolerable. However, it was not until 1948, when the Minneapolis Mayor's Council on Human Relations publicized the endemic prejudice in the city, that jobs in banking, insurance, teaching, and dental hygiene became available to Jewish women.

Jewish women of the region worked in factories during World War II, while more than one hundred entered all branches of the armed forces. Like most middle-class women, they voluntarily stopped working, or were forced to, following demobilization. They rarely reentered the work force once they had children, and then only as part-timers. This pattern of retirement after the birth of children persisted in the region's Jewish communities until the 1970s. Only 1 percent of Minneapolis Jewish mothers worked outside the home in 1971, but nationally more than 50 percent of mothers held jobs that year. The effects of the women's liberation movement that began in the early 1970s, combined with the need for two salaries in order to support a middle-class life-style, led

---

*However, W. Gunther Plaut, *The Jews in Minnesota: The First Seventy-five Years* (New York: American Jewish Historical Society, 1959), 274, footnote, reports that there were two Jewish high school teachers in Minneapolis at that time.

many women once again to expect to work for most of their lives. Family-owned businesses were much rarer in the 1990s than earlier in the century, but the spectrum of job options had widened considerably. As a group, Jewish women had higher educational achievements than the general population. Many chose professions such as medicine, law, accounting, and communications. Others were artists, caterers, and travel agents, while social work and

Social work continues to attract many Jewish women, such as Sharon Friedman, right. Among its various tasks, the Minneapolis Jewish Family and Children's Service sees to the religious needs of its clients.

Blanche Colman, shown here in the 1970s, was South Dakota's first female lawyer.

teaching still attracted significant numbers. The heavy Russian immigration that commenced in the early 1970s added a number of engineers, computer programmers, musicians, and teachers to the regional work force.

.

The career of Blanche Colman is emblematic both of the possibilities open to Jewish working women in the Upper Midwest and of the limitations the region has often placed on Jewish life. Her immigrant father arrived in Deadwood in 1877, soon opened a store, and became active in politics. In 1911 she was the first female admitted to the South Dakota Bar. She spent most of her working life as an attorney for the Homestake Mining Company. Blanche spoke excellent Yiddish and observed many Jewish rituals and customs. Although able to make the leap from immigrant daughter to professional woman, she saw her own Jewish community disappear. She died in 1978 and was buried in the Jewish section of the Deadwood cemetery—probably the last burial that section will receive.

VOICES

OLD COUNTRY/NEW COUNTRY

Ethel Krochock Bernstein's grandmother Shana Gitl was a spinner, herbalist, and midwife. Beginning in 1890 the family migrated in stages from Kresilev, a Ukrainian town near Kiev, to Grand Forks. Though she never learned her new country's language, her skills translated all the same.

My grandmother . . . delivered me. She tied my umbilical cord, and when the doctor arrived and saw what she had done, he said, "very good grandma." When medicine was needed for various ailments my grandmother was taken to the drug store, and, incidentally she couldn't speak or understand English, was taken to a back room of the drug store where many herbs . . . were in jars on shelves. . . . [W]hen she looked them over she pointed to this one and that one, and took the herbs home and either ground or cooked them and made the medicine needed, and they always did the work expected of them.

FARMING ON THE PLAINS

Ethel Schlasinger Overby's parents, having fled Odessa, began farming in North Dakota in 1906. Her mother, Sarah, was unprepared for life on the land.

Sarah had seen farming close at hand as a child in Zebricov [near Odessa], but life on the prairie was much more strenuous than she had imagined. . . . She raised chickens and cared for a garden, cooked and sewed, and worked at heavy labor—welldigging, raking hay in the blazing sun until she almost fainted, following Noah across the prairie as he dug up rocks, then loading them onto the stone boat that the horses would haul to a ravine. . . . When Noah went to work on a road-building crew in the summer, she and her cousin Becky . . . took her cookstove, a cow, dishes and pots, and set up a kitchen in an empty house near the road job. There they fed a hungry crew of 15 men, baking fresh bread every day. When the road job was completed, each of the cooks had earned $30.

———

Celia Kamins was born in New York City around the turn of the century. After the early death of her father, her mother remarried and moved to a North Dakota farm. Celia and her sister, Pearl, joined their mother and stepfather in about 1912.

We dug more rocks on 320 acres than I think they dug in the whole Negev in Israel. We would work all day digging rocks, loading them on stone boats. Somehow or other we assumed that that was the way things had to be. We would quit at four . . . go in and clean up and get ready to milk the cows . . . and my stepbrother and I would milk twenty cows. We separated all that milk with a hand separator. We would carry the cream down in a dugout to keep it from souring. And when it would sit we would skim the cream off the top; use the sour milk for cheese, the cream for butter, and then in the evening when the sun was almost down, but it was still light enough to see, we would pick weeds in the garden and pump water [for] the garden. . . . I was almost a dropout in school because there were only certain days that I could go to school. I couldn't go on Monday because I had to help my mother wash clothes. I couldn't go on Tuesday because we had to iron and bake. I would go Wednesday and Thursday, but Friday I had to stay out because we had to clean house and bake for the weekend.

DAIRY FARMING

Before immigrating, some Russian women had kept cows. Those who could obtain loans to buy cows could continue dairying in America. Abe and Sarah Cohen bought a farm near Duluth in about 1907, their daughter Ida Cohen Golberg recalled.

My mother would make cheese . . . and I watched her. . . . She would put it in jars and leave it sour and skim off that cream and then she would put it on the stove. After awhile it would [thicken,] and after that she put it into a little sackalah [sack] that she made out of a flour sack with a corner, and it would come down into a point and it would drain all the water from the cheese so it would become solid.

———

Two recollections, by Ralph Stacker and Rose Gillman, about St. Paul's West Side, probably dating from the 1920s, attest to the fact that cow-keeping was not restricted to rural areas.

RS: [The husband] wouldn't work . . . so his wife had to support the family. So she bought a cow and she milked the cow, made cottage cheese, made sour cream, delivered it herself. . . . They had a little bit of a shack near the river, and on a winter night . . . they would bring that big—the cow would freeze—they brought the cow in the kitchen. And she supported the family.

RG: [She] had a house full of children and she kept cows . . . and she milked the cows and bottled the milk herself, and went around on a little wagon and delivered it herself. She was always in a hurry, she had so many things to do. And when she went to the butcher's, no matter how many there were standing and waiting in line, he would say, "Lady, you will have to give up your turn for this woman. She is very busy and she doesn't have time to waste." And he would give her a little package of meat and she would run.

SALES WORK AND HELPING OUT

Bessie Halpern was fourteen when her family arrived in Minneapolis in 1900. About three years later, while working at the Leader Department Store, she sought a job at the elegant Young-Quinlan Company, located on the downtown area's prime shopping street.

I ventured out and became a Cash girl. In those days, for a foreign girl . . . this achievement was a big feather in my cap. . . . Time continued, and so did my job and I became a clerk at The Leader Department store in the ready-to-wear apparel. . . . [Some time later] I didn't get any raise in my weekly pay. . . and I became tired of constant promises. At that point, I took courage and went out to one of the finest stores on Nicollet Avenue, The Young-Quinlan Company. I felt I could always put over a good sale on clothes, and why not work in a fancy store with more pay. . . . Other girls could speak English better, but I had the courage. It took nerve to ask, and to my surprise, I was told they would let me know soon. A few days later, back at my usual job at The Leader, a Special Delivery Boy came looking for Miss Halpern. To my surprise, the floorwalker . . . said, "If Young's are after you, we won't let you go." . . . He said that in the next pay check a raise would show up—so I stayed and got $10 a week instead of $6.

Mochel and David Schloff serving Indian customers in their Hazen, North Dakota, general store, about 1925

After marrying Max Schwartz in 1908, Bessie found a different sort of environment in the Belfield, North Dakota, store her husband bought. Belfield was a busy, mixed-nationality market town of five hundred, located on the Northern Pacific line.

During these days, many foreign people traded with us; Ukrainians, Bohemians, Russians, Germans, and Scandinavians. . . . We listened to all the folks' tales of their family problems, and sickness [and] became friends with our customers. In the back of the store, we allotted a space for the farm trade to make and serve themselves with their own lunches; it was a help for them with all their babies. [I] played the sales lady in the store. . . . I was dressed up. I was busy but it was a sort of recreation too, until it was time to make the supper.

———

Belle Woolpy Rauch was born in Russia in 1888 and arrived in Minneapolis with her family at age two. She graduated from high school, and although she was denied a chance for higher education—unlike her brother—she soon found her niche. She took the unusual step of moving from higher status bookkeeping down to sales. This work suited her gregarious nature, and the pay was probably better.

[My] dad had a very peculiar notion . . . girls shouldn't be too well educated. . . . So I went to work at a fur store as a bookkeeper. . . . But I *loved* the selling. . . . And after a while I was on the floor all the time. . . . [We had customers,] "sporting women" and it was so interesting. One had a diamond here, and one had a diamond there . . . in their teeth! That was the style. And they would come in when they needed furs. They were lovely people, as far as we were concerned . . . very easy to sell to, so it was great.

ENTREPRENEURIAL ACTIVITY

In 1909 Lena Kopelman, the mother of six children and pregnant, became widowed. Fortunately, as her daughter Jeanette Kopelman Saval related, she had a business that she continued to expand.

My mother . . . managed with her ability and talent as a wig maker and maker of hair switches and other hair goods. . . . [She] taught us all how to weave human hair and we became fairly adept at it, but we never could make our fingers fly like our mother did. . . .

Kopelman's Beauty Shop was one of the very first beauty shops in Fargo. No license was needed to operate and Rose, Dorothy and I helped to make the shop a going business, all of us merely helping our mother who was quite a business woman. She also went into theatrical supplies and masquerade costumes.

———

Fannie Overman and her family arrived in Superior, Wisconsin, from Russia in about 1904, when she was two. Fannie completed a

Lena Kopelman owned a successful hair-goods company in Fargo, North Dakota, early in the century.

commercial course and worked as a stenographer in Duluth before marrying Abe Goldfine in 1922. As her son Manley related, she was her husband's full partner in a series of rurally based family enterprises.

My dad would buy cattle in the country that he would ship to the South Saint Paul stock yards and then call my mother and say, "cover the checks." She would have to go to the bank . . . or exchange checks with friends and relatives which was quite normal in those days. Since the day they were married, she was completely in charge of all financial arrangements.

After she was married . . . she bought a mailing list of all the farmers in Northern Minnesota. She wrote . . . telling them the Goldfine's Stable had excellent cows and horses for sale. . . .

Fannie weighed 99 pounds . . . and looked very young. Farmers would come to the door . . . and say, "Is your father home?" . . . The farmers would come usually around lunch, so she would make them lunch and then would type up the . . . sales contract.

Between 1932 and 1936 they opened their first feed, seed, and farm supply store. . . . She continued to do all the financing, check writing, paying of bills, etc. . . .

[S]he went to Minneapolis in 1934 for the opening of the bids for the furnishing of horses to the CCC [Civilian Conservation Corps] camps. This was the type of activity she got very much involved in because it took expertise in bookkeeping, financial,

Fannie Goldfine, an outstanding businesswoman in Duluth, at the groundbreaking for her discount store, 1961

and office skills. During the war they couldn't get farm machinery [to sell] so Fannie put in a little furniture department in the machinery warehouse. In 1941–1945 that aspect of business grew. . . .

In 1960–1962 we decided to build a new discount store. . . . [When secondary financing] backed out, Fannie, based on her character and creditability . . . was able to arrange . . . financing . . . [with]in 48 hours. . . . The store was built and in 1962. . . . Fannie stood at the door for 30 days greeting every customer who came in.

BOARDING

The Levin family arrived in Fargo from the Kovno region of Lithuania in 1903. Although Philip was a paperhanger, his wife, Sarah, needed to work as well to help support their five children. Their daughter Rose recalled the roomers the family took in.

My parents . . . purchased a building at 98 Front St. where they opened a confectionery store and rooming house. We lived in rooms in back of the store, and the roomers lived upstairs. Our roomers consisted of railroad workers, lumber jacks and farm hands. . . .

[Years later] mother was anxious to get us away from Front St. and the gentile roomers when we girls became teenagers, so she sold the store and moved . . . into an apartment building.

————

Cecyle Eirinberg Marsh lived in Delmont, South Dakota, where her father owned a store during the late 1920s.

We boarded three schoolteachers in Delmont beside four children, so [mother] didn't work in the store. Without the schoolteachers we wouldn't have existed.

————

Warsaw-born Sam Char arrived in St. Paul in 1913 along with several of his companions after being laid off from railroad work in Omaha. They all needed rooms and, with the aid of a female friend, went out looking for them on the largely Jewish West Side.

The woman . . . said to us, "as you can see I cannot keep you here, but in the next block [Fairfield Avenue] I know at least 6 women who have extra room, and they would be happy and glad each one of them to take on one roomer." . . . The lady put on a long wool shawl over her shoulder and told us to take our suitcases & by noon time she had located us all with different families and the room rent was five dollars per month.

FACTORY WORK

Recollections of Upper Midwestern factory work in written and oral sources are rare because relatively few Jewish women in the region held such jobs for very long in the late 1800s and early 1900s. Sarah Yager arrived from the Ukraine with her parents in 1889, at eighteen months of age. When she was ten she began working full time: Her father had deserted the family, and her mother was ailing. Sherna Shalett Vinograd, Sarah's daughter, tells the story.

Sarah left school for a job in a pants factory. The employment of ten-year-olds was beginning to be illegal. Sometimes she had to be hidden from the government inspector. She remembered this incident. "All of a sudden a man comes, and the owner comes. He throws a whole bunch of pants on top of me and sits on them, and he says, "Goddammit, get that inspector out of here, or I'll smother this child." . . . I pulled bastings . . . [for] $1.50 a week. . . . [I worked f]rom Monday to Saturday, seven o'clock in the morning to six . . . at night.

———

Edith Modelevsky reached America with her mother and siblings in 1922. She quit school after a year, at age fifteen, to "help out at home [and] . . . become more independent."

A neighbor by the name of Ben worked for H. Lang Manufacturing Company in South St. Paul. They manufactured overalls, coveralls and jackets. The neighbor took me there and did a bit of lying. He told them I was sixteen, not fifteen, and that I was his sister. They gave me a job. . . . I sewed the zippers on overall pants. . . . It was all piecework, and we were paid according to how much we did. I was fast and I wanted to make as much money as possible. The moment I finished a bundle, I would rush over to get another one. After a while, I was making $25 a week, which was a lot of money in those days. There were men in the factory, some of them married, who made only $12 a week.

———

Her daughter Slovie Solomon Apple related how Clara Rothman got her first job as a needleworker in Minneapolis in 1912. She was seventeen and had been taught her skills at home in Rumania. Her fiancé spoke English and accompanied her to job interviews that had been arranged by a local Jewish organization. Garment-industry working conditions were evidently no better in the Twin Cities than in New York City.

A St. Paul hat factory that employed many Jewish men and women, about 1920

Ladies' fashions at this time were beautiful blouses and dresses made of the finest fabrics. There was a great demand for fine seamstresses in shops and factories in what was known as the needle-and-thread trade.

One of Clara's interviews included a test of hand-sewing the finishing touches on a collar on a silk dress. She got the job the following week. She did all the fine hand-stitching on the most delicate fabrics, like silks, georgettes, and fine linens. It was painstaking work, but she sewed with the skill of an artist. . . .

Each girl was given a quota every day and had to finish it and sometimes even do extra pieces or lose her job. Sometimes the young women were ill and couldn't finish their quotas. They helped each other out, skipping their fifteen-minute lunch breaks and doing the extra pieces. They all needed this support system at one time or another. . . . Working conditions were far from good. In summer the rooms were too warm and the girls left their sewing tables only once during the day—for a drink of water. Lighting was better in summer. . . . In the winter the lighting was very poor. Ceiling lights hung down, but not far enough. One bulb hanging from an electric cord didn't cast much light. The room was cold, warmed by one heater in a far corner.

Clara said years later, "My feet were so cold, I couldn't feel them to push down the pedal on the sewing machine."

Sometimes the girls' fingers were so cold, they could hardly hold the needles. Clara's eyes were becoming strained, and she had great difficulty seeing in the winter.

A few years later, her first marriage foundered. Clara supported her three daughters by dressmaking, working out of her apartment.

During the recession that followed World War I, she sold her wares door to door. Her vision began to fail, and she was advised to give up needlework. In desperation, she took a job in a South St. Paul meat-packing plant. The eldest child, five-year-old Slovie, was left in charge of her middle sister. The baby was taken to a neighbor.

It was low-paying [work] . . . that employed mostly immigrant women. . . . Clara and the other women worked in a large, very cold, damp room. The floors were always wet, and the women wore rubbers and stood on wooden planks, raised one inch off the floor. The damp cold penetrated deep into every bone of their bodies.

Their job was stuffing sausage skins as fast as they could. They were paid by the hour, but quotas for the hour had to be met. Working conditions were deplorable, but there were no complaints. With the scarcity of jobs and hundreds lined up for every one available, a person considered himself fortunate to have one of any kind.

The women had to pay for their white uniforms and were required to wear a fresh one every day. Clara could only afford one, so it had to be laundered and ironed every night. . . . Clara often came home so nauseous she couldn't eat. She had been inhaling the foul stench [from the meat-packing plant] all day . . . and [it] made her ill.

WHITE-COLLAR WORK

Secretarial and bookkeeping work generally required special training and thus conferred status. However, wits could suffice. Sarah Yager Shalett left her job at a Minneapolis pants factory after about a year. At fifteen she learned to dress hair and do manicures. Then, in about 1904, she found a new job.

When I was sixteen, my dear friend said to me . . . "We need a bookkeeper." "I don't know anything about bookkeeping," I said. "But you're good at figures" [, she replied]. Anyway, she convinced me I should come. [Sarah noticed a $1,000 mistake in the books when being interviewed and was hired.] I started that job at $18.00 a week. This almost killed my friend; she was getting $15 and she was a graduate of business college.

———

Four months after Edith Modelevsky started work at St. Paul's H. Lang Manufacturing Company, in about 1925, she was offered an office job. Although the salary was lower, she took the position and received raises. A year later she decided to invest in further training.

I was really interested in learning so I could make a better living for myself. . . . I enrolled in Globe Business College to learn shorthand, typing, business English and bookkeeping. . . . I learned how to operate all the machines at the company [where she worked], and I often went into the factory to show a newly-hired person how to run a particular machine.

———

During the 1930s some business schools refused to train Jewish girls, as the nineteen-year-old Fannie Schwartz of Minneapolis found out.

I wanted to attend a specific business machine school. . . . In those days if a girl finished comptometer school she earned $35 a week, big money. I was received by this lovely looking Nordic, I'm being polite, and she had my name on there, asked me to sit down, and started asking questions about experience and grades in school and what I hoped to do. Then she said, "I have just one last question to ask you. Are you Jewish?" And I said, "Yes." And after a pause she said to me, "We don't have any Jewish students." I said, "I'm sorry about that. I don't mind being the only one." She said, "We don't place Jewish students." And I said, "You don't have to place me; just train me. I'll get my own job." And she paused, and pretty soon she said, "I'm sorry, but I can't accept you or your money." And that was the end of the conversation. My money was returned to me, pushed back across the desk and I was asked to leave the office.

TEACHING

Augusta Machowsky and Abraham Pomerance met in Brooklyn, New York, where their parents shared a house. Both families had emigrated from southern Russia in about 1900 and became dissatisfied with the East Coast. They moved first to Grand Forks, North Dakota, and then took out homestead claims near the town of Lehr. Augusta and Abe were left in Brooklyn to finish high school. Arriving in North Dakota in about 1908 but not yet married, their daughter Rita Pomerance Gusack reported many years later, they were hired as teachers—but at separate schools.

After my mother and father got to North Dakota . . . they were both asked to teach school. . . . [H]ers was #3, and since it was quite a way from the family homestead, she lived during the week with a German family named Kapline, in Lehr. . . . Mother is about 4 feet 8 inches tall and some of the pupils in her class were in their 20's and more than a foot taller than she, and gave her many hard times, especially since some of them spoke no English. At one point, in 1910 there was such a blizzard after school started that she decided that even though the only heat in the school house was from a pot bellied stove, that it was safer to keep the children in school than send them home. One father came after his children in a horse and buggy and she argued with him not to go home, but he paid no attention. She and the rest of the class stayed at school with no food, water only from snow, and little heat for 3 days until my father arrived with help. Later that day they found the father . . . frozen to death with his children.

————

Frances Halpern graduated from the University of Minnesota in 1924 with a degree in education. Her sister, Blanche, recalled how desperate Frances was to find a job.

Rhoda Redleaf teaching a nursery
school class at the St. Paul Jewish
Community Center, 1969

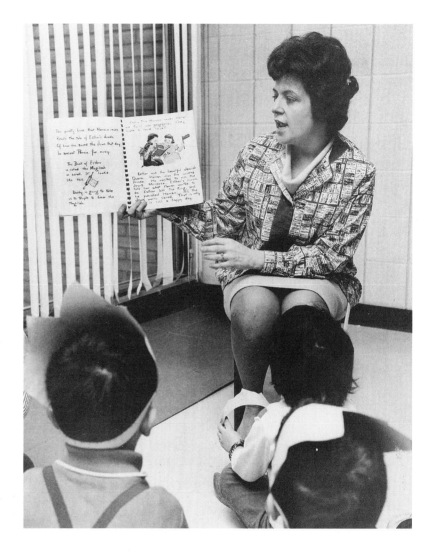

The University maintains it gets you a job to teach when you
get through. And every time [Frances] was interviewed by a principal, [the question would be] "And what is your religion?" And
when she said, "Jewish" . . . that would interfere. . . . My sister
became desperate and she finally wrote a letter to [a friend] . . .
teaching in Grand Rapids, Minnesota. She said, "How did you
get your job[?] It seems that I can't get a job because I am

Jewish." . . . He answered "You'll get a job. Just don't answer that question. Put anything down but Jewish." And sure enough as soon . . . as there was another possibility she put down Unitarian. What else could she do?

———

Sara Bashefkin Ryder was born on St. Paul's West Side in 1906 and worked as a clerk in a grocery store before attending St. Cloud Teachers' College (now St. Cloud State University); she graduated in 1928. She was rejected by several rural schools because she was Jewish and finally found a position in a remote northern part of the state.

To get to Nemadji, one had to go by bus to Barnum, Minnesota, and then get someone to drive you four and one half miles to Nemadji. . . . [We] three teachers lived in the teacherage, a frail two story house about 100 feet from the school. . . . We had outside plumbing . . . [and] we had to get our kerosene outside from a tank. . . . It was not too easy . . . [c]oming from large cities. . . . However, we all stuck it out for two years, patiently waiting to return to civilization and home.

———

Dorothy Mosow Hurwitz grew up in Alcester, South Dakota, and Sioux City, Iowa, during the 1920s.

I went two years to Morningside College, and then I went one year to the Pestalozzi Froebel Teachers College in Chicago. [Johann Pestalozzi and Friedrich Froebel were European educational innovators.] And I got my three year teaching diploma, went back to Sioux City (in 1930–1931) [but] couldn't get a job. So I opened up my own nursery school in my parents' home. And had the nursery school until the time we were married in 1934. [My husband was attending law school at the University of Iowa.] . . . I taught at the U. of Iowa nursery school, and went back to school and got my degree in education.

———

Eva Levy was born in Grand Forks, North Dakota, in 1899. Soon after, her father bought a store in Wells, Minnesota.

I . . . attended Miss Wood's kindergarten training school in Minneapolis [then] taught school in Wells, Minnesota, where my parents lived until 1921. My father died suddenly. In the fall of 1921, my mother and I moved to St. Paul. I started working for the Jewish Family Welfare [Association] in January, 1922. I had no social work training but . . . I worked part time and attended the University of Minnesota. . . . This was during the time of a large Russian immigration. . . . I practically learned to speak Yiddish. . . . I would accompany [people with health problems] to the Wilder Dispensary [free clinic]. I acted as the interpreter. . . . I also took groups out to the Sophie Wirth camp at White Bear Lake.*

SOCIAL WORK

Ida Blehert Davis described her mother's unofficial but significant career in St. Paul at the turn of the century. Davis herself became a social worker in 1913.

In the meantime, social welfare training along [with] other lines were not neglected at home—At 9 I began making trips to the city hospital with *goldene* chicken soup and noodles for Jewish patients. . . . Also, there (were boarders) more recently arrived immigrants, some of them relatives, who somehow spent their first days at our home—no societies then to set them up in housekeeping, no resettlement committees, no self-support loans—no, instead I accompanied Mother to the Treasurer of the Loan Society where I had to be the interpreter when she borrowed money for her friends and relatives. . . . And what of this other big field of Family casework? Everyone came to our house for personal and financial help. Did Michle lose all her cows?

---

*Sophie Wirth Camp provided a camping experience for the children of Jewish immigrants and had shorter sessions for their mothers as well.

We helped her by buying chickens and eggs. Did Malke have trouble with her straying husband? Did Elka . . . have to run away from her brutal husband? Where did she stay, but at our house. Did little Fanny have to make a living after her husband divorced her and married [a] "Yenke"? Who started her off as a pedler [sic] of notions? . . .

Nor did she confine herself only to our people. . . . How well I remember the colored woman next door whom she befriended, the outcast girl who lived in one of the vacant flats until she found work.

ARMED SERVICES

During World War II more than one hundred Jewish women from the region joined the armed services, working as nurses, dietitians, and machinists, and managing the arrivals, departures, and assignments of thousands of servicemen and servicewomen. In 1942 Laura Rapaport was asked to join the first group trained to become officers in the Women Appointed for Volunteer Emergency Service (WAVES).

When I got that first call asking me if I would be interested in coming into the service they were establishing for women in the Navy, I first was so surprised I just practically flopped. . . . And I began to think, like the philosopher, "If not me, who, if not now, when." Why wouldn't I go, what right had I not to go. Just because I had a job and a nice salary, was that a reason not to go? . . . I did not feel it was incumbent on me to prove my patriotism as a Jew. I felt maybe I could do something. . . . I was concerned about Hitler.

EXPERIENCES OF RECENT RUSSIAN IMMIGRANTS

The saga of immigration and job seeking has continued in recent decades. Russian Jews who began arriving in the 1970s were typically well educated. Those who were engineers or computer programmers were often able to transfer their skills to American jobs.

Sophia Shankman Rosenauer and her family left Leningrad for
St. Paul in 1977.

So I went through the school for five years and got a master's
degree in mechanical engineering. I started to work for one consulting firm in Leningrad. . . . [After I moved to St. Paul] I worked
for Control Data for seven years, . . . and in May 1990 I started
to work for a consulting firm in downtown Minneapolis. . . . And
this is exactly the same [work] I did in Russia.

———

Inna Gendelman Brezman, her husband, Michael, and daughter,
Anna, arrived in the Twin Cities from Leningrad in 1979. She had
been trained as a nurse.

Oh, my adjustment was a little bit more difficult because I
didn't know any English. I had questions of what to do. Felicia
Weingarten arranged a tour for me in a hospital. [Weingarten, a

WAVE Laura Rapaport (center)
attended a Seder at Hunter
College in New York City in
1944. More than one hundred
Jewish women from the Upper
Midwest served in the armed
forces during World War II.

Holocaust survivor who arrived in St. Paul in the late 1940s, befriended Soviet immigrants who moved to that city.] I was terrified. When I saw all the equipment in the American hospitals here, I was absolutely terrified of doing anything near that hospital. Maybe because of the lack of language, maybe because I was overwhelmed with all that high tech. Then I had to go for four years back to school—start all my education over again. . . . So I decided to go to a dental assistant school. . . . I worked with a dentist in downtown St. Paul. . . . After [my daughter] Jessica was born, I didn't stay with it. First of all, because I thought my English didn't improve there at all. You can't talk to people with their mouth open. . . . So I stayed with Jessica for six months at home, and then I went to beauty school, which was only six weeks. I was able to choose my own hours working as a manicurist so I could juggle babysitters and baby. . . . I meet wonderful people every day, and I do blabber a lot. My English improved a lot, to the point that I understand more than my husband does.

CHAPTER FIVE

"We Had to Create It"
Women and Synagogues

One of the things about growing up outside a Jewish community is that I could do whatever I wanted to do as far as whatever I read in books, and I was reading about women in Judaism. I didn't have a community to say, "You can't do that." . . . There are eight of us (Gordon cousins) who grew up in Albert Lea [Minnesota]. We've all married someone Jewish and we all have strong Jewish identities each in different ways. . . . Many of us were looking for something because it didn't exist in Albert Lea and feeling that void we were drawn to Judaism in its many different forms. We didn't take it for granted. We had to create it.

RABBI JULIE GORDON came of age in a small Minnesota town during the 1960s. Her memory of her effort to forge a meaningful spiritual life in a place that lacked a formalized Jewish community is an updated version of the struggle that faced Jews who settled in the Upper Midwest in the late 1800s and early 1900s—how to create a Jewish life where little or none existed. For those immigrants, the struggle involved important questions: How would they maintain Jewish practices, tied as they were to religious law and to compact, organized Jewish communities? How would they resolve the tension between a religion that viewed those born into it as members of a people and the American emphasis on voluntarism and pluralism? Finally, how would women help refashion institutional religious life once they were transplanted to the Upper Midwest? The specific ways all these questions were dealt with depended on the countries immigrants came from, when they arrived, and where they settled— not to mention a complex interplay between evolving Jewish beliefs and practices and American religious and civic life.

.

Amelia Ullmann's reminiscences, written long after she left St. Paul, make no reference to her religion. Yet it was important to her. In August 1859, she buried her child in what was then the only Jewish cemetery in Minnesota. In 1887, some time after she had returned to her native Germany, she sent a Torah scroll and lectern cover to Mount Zion Hebrew Congregation in St. Paul. It is not known whether she embroidered the cover, but it is certain that she could not read the scroll.

Sima Tiba Rudnitsky in her home
in Superior, Wisconsin, late
1930s. Jewish women who had
emigrated from Eastern Europe
often prayed at home.

Jewish women have traditionally played a secondary role within their synagogues. The Torah commands that men pray three
times a day, but it gives no such direction to women. Thus the synagogue has customarily been a male-oriented institution. Traditionally, women were not included in the daily minyan (prayer
quorum), and they were not allowed to hold or read from the
Torah. Their piety was primarily expressed in keeping a kosher
kitchen and in instilling time-honored Jewish values in their children. They could pray at home. When they attended services they
were segregated, usually in a balcony section, where they would not
disturb the devotions of the men. Despite this partitioning, they

made their presence felt and evinced their ties to the synagogue in other ways, such as through monetary donations and gifts of handiwork. This was the situation of women in Europe up to the mid-nineteenth century.

The first Jewish women to settle in the Upper Midwest came from such a world. These were the Germans who founded synagogues such as St. Paul's Mount Zion Hebrew Association (later, Mount Zion Hebrew Congregation) in 1856 and Minneapolis's Shaari Tof (later, Temple Israel) in 1878. At this time synagogues founded by German Jews all over the country were slowly and selectively easing out of orthodoxy and into the Reform movement. In 1878 Mount Zion formally joined the movement, and Shaari Tof began the transition soon after. Reform Judaism stressed the importance of ethical monotheism and denied the age-old validity of Jewish law.* Reform services were more orderly and uniform than in Orthodox synagogues—each member worshiped using the same prayer book. Keeping kosher, the great social separator of Jew from gentile, was now a matter of choice rather than law. Reform adherents in America found that this approach allowed the practice and rites of Judaism to fit more comfortably with those of the nation's Protestant majority. Jewish women, too, found that the American synagogue afforded them new opportunities to enlarge their roles and enhance their status. Taking advantage of these opportunities, they moved beyond the bounds of the synagogue and into the community.

Increasingly in America, German-Jewish women became more regular in their synagogue attendance than men. Here they were fol-

---

*The Reform movement, which originated in northern Germany in the early 1800s, was truly launched in America with the issuing in 1886 of the Pittsburgh Platform, which clearly laid out the distinctions between Reform and the then prevailing and normative Orthodox Judaism. That same year, other rabbis, horrified at what they considered the excesses of Reform, founded the Conservative movement. Like Reform Jews, Conservatives viewed changes in religious expression as normal and necessary, but they laid greater emphasis on tying change to biblical and rabbinic precedent. Orthodox Jews saw the laws and practices of Judaism as binding on every generation. Thus they resisted—and continue to resist—most change.

lowing a path laid down by American Protestant women and their clergy. By the 1830s, it was women who filled the church pews on Sundays. It was women, the clergy proclaimed, who had a special affinity for religious devotion, while men devoted themselves to the earthly world of commerce. As more and more German-Jewish men felt the need to keep stores open on Saturday, in defiance of the commandment to rest on the Sabbath, their wives and children became willing substitutes in the synagogues. Even if women could not follow services in Hebrew very well, they could understand the sermons, which were often preached in German—their native tongue.

Within Reform Judaism, as it was practiced in late-nineteenth-century America, there were other benefits for women. For example, the custom of segregating women had come to be disparagingly viewed as "Oriental": Families now sat together. Women were encouraged to study with the rabbi, Sunday schools were introduced and utilized women as teachers, and new rites, such as the confirmation service, were introduced.

Confirmation is an ancient Christian ceremony. The Reform movement no doubt appropriated elements from Lutheran confirmation practices and reconfigured them to signify Jewish religious adulthood. Unlike the ancient ritual of bar mitzvah, which marks thirteen-year-old males as adults (and which Reform Judaism initially discarded), the confirmation ceremony, which occurred between the ages of fourteen and sixteen, was open to females as well. Its first mention in the Upper Midwest was in the November 12, 1871, board minutes of the St. Paul Mount Zion Hebrew Congregation. That same year, the newly formed Hebrew Ladies Benevolent Society (HLBS) offered to purchase an organ for the congregation. Of interest here is the fact that it was women who pushed for this aesthetic embellishment, while the men hesitated to accept—probably because the organ had long been associated with Christian worship.

It was mainly through the work conducted by women's societies attached to synagogues that women first established their true authority outside the realm of the home. Benevolent societies, as they were then called, had long been associated with American churches, where their function was to help keep church finances healthy and aid members in distress. In German-speaking countries Jewish women were familiar with *vereins* or *khevres* (loosely organized benevolent societies). In the United States they grafted an American Protestant shoot onto the Jewish trunk to create a hybrid. The spirit of this hybrid often was closer to Protestant "charity," with its connotation of the worthiness of those destitute, than to the *khevre*, which had been based on tzedakah (righteousness), signifying an individual and communal obligation to help all Jews in need.

A brief look at the Mount Zion HLBS not only indicates the kind of work such societies performed in Upper Midwestern Reform synagogues during the late nineteenth century but also reflects their

This synagogue for St. Paul's Mount Zion Congregation was constructed in 1902 with considerable help from the Hebrew Ladies Benevolent Society.

Hannah Austrian, a mainstay of the Mount Zion Congregation's Hebrew Ladies Benevolent Society, about 1900

prevailing attitudes. First of all, the HLBS raised money—with great success. A fair the society sponsored in 1902 brought in $11,500 toward the $80,000 cost of constructing a new synagogue building. The society also dispersed its funds widely, to national and local Jewish charities as well as to local secular ones. Money was sent to the Cleveland Jewish Orphan Asylum and the local Jewish Home for the Aged as well as to St. Paul's Free Dispensary, United Charities, and St. Luke's Hospital. The *St. Paul Globe* reported on February 3, 1897, that "During the last year . . . the Hebrews of the city, through this society, contributed half of the money given to charity in St. Paul," even though Jews only made up one-tenth of the recipients.

It was in attending to local Jewish needs, however, that the HLBS made its greatest contribution. Through the society, members set the stamp of their concern for the welfare of women and children upon the present and the future. Indeed, the HLBS was the forerunner of many existing Jewish social-service agencies in St. Paul. A few examples from its records illustrate how the society changed its programs, and even its name, to serve the developing Jewish community.

The HLBS had been formed with the chartered purpose of ministering to families in need. Within the congregation, it appears to have acted as an informal loan society, too. For a decade, both the grantors and grantees were predominantly German Jews. But the sudden flood of immigration precipitated by fierce pogroms in Russia changed that.

Once Eastern European Jews began arriving in St. Paul, the HLBS sprang into action. The women acted as "friendly visitors" who ascertained whether newcomers were truly "destitute and worthy" of receiving assistance. If they were, the HLBS responded, paying for such necessities as coal, new eyeglasses, hospital bills, and even train fare to other cities. Society members also found Jewish homes for orphans who had been sent to the state facility in Owatonna and continued checking on them for years afterward. In addition, the HLBS loaned money to sundry industrious Jews for such things as peddlers' licenses, horses, sewing machines, and goods to sell.

Of much more lasting importance than face-to-face charity was the HLBS's founding of institutions such as the Industrial School, which soon became the Neighborhood House, a settlement house on St. Paul's West Side.* In 1903 it was reorganized along nonsectarian lines so that it could better serve all the ethnic groups residing in that part of the city. Despite this change, Mount Zion congregants continued to serve actively on the board. Like other American settlement houses, Neighborhood House offered educational, social, and recreational activities as well as citizenship classes to the Jewish, Polish, Syrian, and, later, Mexican inhabitants of the West Side.

In 1901 the HLBS split into two organizations, the Temple Guild, whose function was to support the synagogue, and the Jewish Relief Society (JRS), which addressed social needs. The JRS founded a day nursery on the West Side for working mothers, and it ran an employment bureau that found work for immigrant mothers, some no doubt in factories owned by members' husbands. Additionally, in 1912, the JRS established the Lake Rest Vacation Camp at White Bear Lake "for the benefit of over-worked and tired Jewish mothers and their children."

Minneapolis had its HLBS-JRS counterpart in the Baszion Benevolent Society, which was named for its founder, Shaari Tof member Baszion Rees. She established it in 1876 to fund her nascent congregation's cemetery association.† However, the society soon began offering nonsectarian aid to the poor and sick. Renamed the Temple Israel Auxiliary in 1903, it dutifully helped pay the mortgage, furnish, and provide flowers for the substantial new

---

*The society's minutes indicate that in 1895 it donated "one hundred dollars to the . . . woman's Council for the purpose of organizing an 'Industrial School.'" The "woman's Council" referred to was the local chapter of the National Council of Jewish Women (NCJW), which had recently been organized in the city by Rachel Haas, a Mount Zion congregant and HLBS member. The NCJW's membership was virtually identical to that of the HLBS. For decades, NCJW meetings were held in the synagogue's vestry rooms.

†It was not uncommon for women's benevolent societies to be formed before churches or synagogues were built. Likewise, cemetery land was often purchased before buildings were acquired.

building that was finished a year later. By the beginning of the century, Duluth's Temple Emanuel also had a women's auxiliary that did much the same work by providing funds for the synagogue and by looking after and helping to Americanize Jewish immigrants in the port city.

Although most synagogue women's societies' time was devoted to fund-raising and benevolent works, study was not forgotten. In 1897, for example, Mount Zion's Rabbi Emanuel Hess conducted courses in ethics and biblical prophets for his female congregants, while his daughter, Julia, led a study circle and taught Sunday school.

·

The various developments sketched above make it clear that Reform-movement women—in the Upper Midwest and around the nation—were entering new areas of service at a time when their religiosity was no longer primarily tied to keeping kosher. They were being accorded a place at the study table and were allowed to teach as well (although they were not allowed into the Reform seminary). They were important as worshipers, as fund-raisers, and as succorers of the needy. In the latter role they had moved well beyond the sphere of their homes and synagogues and into the civic arena. By describing their work, however, in a language that fused caring for one's family with caring for society's unfortunates, both women and men could overlook some rather profound changes that were occurring in prescribed gender roles.

The Russian Jews who began arriving in the Upper Midwest in the early 1880s came from a culture in which gender roles were rigidly defined. In creating synagogues in the new land, they faced the considerable challenge of sustaining these roles—not to mention the rest of their worshiping traditions—in settings that might best be termed rough-and-ready.

Jewish farmers in North and South Dakota rarely purchased buildings to serve as synagogues; their tenancy on the land was too transient for that. Instead they concerned themselves first with

The Sunshine Club of Virginia, Minnesota, 1909. Like the Bikur Kholim, this group's function was to visit the sick.

buying cemetery land, a more pressing necessity. They generally met for worship at the largest local farmhouse—with the most learned farmer leading services. Men and women sat apart as usual, but even at this early stage, that separation was not hard and fast. The small synagogues of Ashley and Wishek, North Dakota, in use during the 1920s, had no women's balconies.

The situation was different in larger towns. While prayer spaces remained segregated, congregations soon learned that in America they could not get along without a Ladies' Aid Society (LAS)—to help construct or purchase, and to furnish, the building they all ultimately required. These societies, like those established by German-Jewish women, had their roots partially in Old Country institutions. Eastern European Jewish women learned from their Reform

Sarah Lee Ginsberg embroidered this Torah mantle in 1930 when an uncle, Harry Ginsberg, presented B'nai Israel Congregation of Grand Forks, North Dakota, with a Torah scroll.

counterparts how to modernize the *khevre* and make it serve new functions in America.

Women eagerly fell to the task of raising funds for new synagogues. Of course, women paid for equipping the kitchen that was part of any American synagogue. They were not shy about deciding how certain portions of the money they brought in would be spent, either. In 1909, for example, the LAS of B'nai Abraham synagogue in Virginia, Minnesota, turned $700 over to the men and moved that the congregation "furnish a Ladies' Aid Window." When they attended services, the ladies of Virginia could view from the balcony the lovely stained-glass window they had purchased. Financial support did not translate into increased participation in the religious services, and custom dictated that women be out of the male worshipers' sight. In Virginia, young women were not even hired to teach Sunday school until the 1930s. There were no fixed rules regarding teaching, however, and some synagogues were relatively open to change. For instance, in the 1910s the Orthodox Kenesseth Israel congregation in Minneapolis hired Eleanore H. Bresky, who later became an ardent suffragist, to teach Sunday school.

These societies, in general, also served as benevolent associations. As had the *khevres*, they supplied matzohs to poorer Jews at Passover and looked after their needs throughout the year. The societies contributed to the various funds set up to aid victims of Russian pogroms, and during World War I they aided the American Red Cross. In the synagogue itself, women's money generally went for repairs and furnishings but also for smaller items such as children's gifts and holiday treats.

Women in Orthodox synagogues were not all recent immigrants, unsophisticated, or lacking in means. By 1899, women in Orthodox benevolent societies in St. Paul such as the Sisters of Peace and the Bikur Kholim (visiting the sick) joined with women representing Mount Zion's Jewish Relief Society to create a citywide United Jewish Charities organization affiliated with the National Conference of Jewish Charities; this was the first (albeit short-lived) attempt to unify the delivery of Jewish social services locally. Additionally, in 1906 the Sisters of Peace and the Charity Loan Society

Synagogue auxiliaries like the one that served St. Paul's Temple of Aaron staged numerous patriotic pageants during the 1940s.

founded the city's Jewish Home for the Aged. Adas Israel Ladies' Aid of Duluth and the Sisters of Peace in Minneapolis are other examples of Orthodox synagogue women's groups that helped the poor, the sick, and the needy as well as their own synagogues.

The formation of the successful Jewish Charities in 1910 and the hiring of a paid social worker signaled the coming trend in women's philanthropy: professionalization and the attendant separation of social service from synagogue. The evolution of group names—from "benevolent society" and "Ladies' Aid" to the more recent "Women's League" and "sisterhood"—reflects this change. The Women's League for Conservative Judaism offers a good example of how these formal names signified new functions.

The Women's League was founded in New York City in 1918 by Mathilda Schechter, wife of the chancellor of the Jewish Theological Seminary there. The seminary was, and still is, the main training ground for rabbis, cantors, and teachers who serve the Conservative movement. Schechter saw a need for a national women's organization that promoted unity, piety, education, and aesthetics.

The Women's League affiliated with Adath Jeshurun synagogue in Minneapolis was a charter chapter; within ten years, two additional chapters were formed in St. Paul and Minneapolis. The Conservative movement appealed to women who had been raised in Orthodox homes but wanted a modern setting in which to worship. The Conservative synagogues offered mixed seating, which allowed women to sit with their families. Also, the rabbis appreciated female attendance at services. Rabbis in fact encouraged women to enroll in study sessions, recognizing that many had received a poor religious education and that the move to America had often disrupted the customary handing down from mothers to daughters of religious lore. Conservative synagogues also had no qualms about hiring women to teach in their Sunday schools. With a nod to the Reform movement, they also instituted the Confirmation service.

Upper Midwestern Women's League chapters undertook a wide range of functions, including, for instance, forming Red Cross units

Confirmation class, Sioux Falls,
South Dakota, about 1925

The women's auxiliary of B'nai Israel Congregation, Sioux Falls, South Dakota, preparing for a synagogue dinner, about 1950

during World War II. The greater part of their activities, however, were aimed at benefiting the synagogue and, indirectly, the home. They all shouldered traditional responsibilities, which included synagogue beautification, fund-raising, and support of children's programs. For example, during the 1950s and 1960s Minneapolis's Beth El synagogue Women's League underwrote that congregation's religious school, founded and oversaw the operation of its nursery school, supported its library, and helped raise funds to build a dormitory at the Jewish Theological Seminary to house women studying to become Hebrew-school teachers. In addition, the Beth El Women's League sponsored congregational dinners and baked for after-service social hours. It also raised money by holding rummage and bake sales, by selling advertisements, by staging revues, theatrical events, and style shows, and by cooking and serving countless dinners. Every synagogue auxiliary did this sort of work. So, for that matter, did every church women's group.

There was a particular area in which the Women's League was of immense importance. It educated its members to be standard-bearers of an American Judaism, one that mixed Jewish tradition with secular national styles of modernity and abundance. Keeping a kosher home was encouraged, but the aesthetics surrounding the holiday celebrations were to be American. Perhaps the best example of this new mode of observance was the "Jewish Home Beautiful," a program promoted by the national Women's League headquarters in New York City that combined a printed holiday-observance guide with a synagogue pageant. First presented in 1941, it was revived countless times during the next thirty or so years. In the pageant, the stage was set with a grouping of bounteously laid holiday tables. As the spotlight fell on each in turn, a woman narrator provided the given holiday's history, describe how it was presently being celebrated, and tell what foods to serve. After the narrator spoke, another woman sang traditional melodies specific to the holiday. The accompanying printed guide offered further examples for elegant table settings and

A "Jewish Home Beautiful" program demonstrating a Sabbath table setting, St. Paul, 1940s

gave recipes for traditional foods. This presentation was so popular that it was taken up by every synagogue auxiliary across the Jewish spectrum; and it was particularly successful as an interfaith program. It explained Jewish holiday customs and imparted a visual reassurance that the settings and foods were not too "foreign."

With the general postwar move to the suburbs, many sisterhoods shouldered new fund-raising responsibilities. Perhaps the most interesting fund-raiser was the synagogue gift shop. Originally it sold utilitarian items, like a Jewish subset of a dry-goods store. The stock customarily included candlesticks for use on Friday evening, menorahs and candles for Chanukah, Seder plates for Passover, kiddush cups, and religious books. After World War II, however, the gift shop grew far beyond the filling of these simple needs. It came to present itself as a variety of boutique, and its abundance of goods helped create a new consumption-oriented Jewish identity. A panoply of brass and copper Israeli-made products, such as Seder plates and Chanukah menorahs, began being imported during the 1950s and 1960s, and Jewish families could, by buying these and other items, express their pride in and identify with those Jews who were rebuilding the ancient homeland. By the 1970s, fine British and American china products made expressly for the Jewish holidays joined the Israeli objects. Today, Lucite trays and bookends engraved with Jewish symbols are sold as wedding and bar and bat mitzvah gifts, as well as menorahs in the shape of television stars such as Barney the dinosaur. The message is that one can be both Jewish and modern, ethnic and American, upper middle class and, somehow, an Israeli pioneer. The macrocosm is American consumerism; the microcosm is nothing less than a redefinition of what it means to be an American Jew. As family purchasing agent and cultural arbiter, the woman has been given a powerful say in this refashioning of identity.

•

As consumers women had an important role to play. Through the programs, lectures, and gift shops they sponsored, their cultural authority was enormous. As fund-raisers and cooks, their involvement was critical. But on the bimah (the pulpit area), until the mid-1970s, their presence was still minuscule. They were generally absent but for one evening a year, set aside as a "Sisterhood Sabbath." Even this event was generally made part of the Friday-night service, which does not have the same aura of holiness as the Saturday-morning service, when the Torah is read.*

At Women's League conventions—the yearly regional one and the biennial national one—women led services and even read from the Torah. But at their own synagogues they were not accorded these privileges. It was true that between the 1920s and the mid-1940s, girls in the Conservative movement could celebrate a bat mitzvah modified to fit into the Friday-night service.† They could also ascend the bimah during Confirmation ceremonies. That, however, was generally the extent of female involvement in the sacred space. There is no recorded indication that area women or their daughters were upset about this imbalance. Instead it was Twin Cities Conservative rabbis who found the absence of females on the bimah on Saturday morning problematic. In the mid-1940s they began encouraging thirteen-year-old girls to fulfill the bat mitzvah by being called up, like their brothers, to read from the Torah on Saturday. During this same time, the bat mitzvah was starting to

*It was the Conservative movement that was formulating a new role for women within the sacred service. Women in the Reform movement had by the early twentieth century achieved what sociologist Marshall Sklare termed "formal equality coupled with limited participation." For example, although the national Reform seminary in Cincinnati, Ohio, balked at ordaining female rabbis. Orthodox Jews continue to hold fast to the traditional roles of men and women.

†The first bat mitzvah ceremony was conducted on the East Coast in 1922. That year Sarah Berman, then president of the Minneapolis Talmud Torah, wrote in the September 22 issue of the Twin Cities newspaper *American Jewish World*: "[M]ention should be made of an innovation introduced by a representative of the women for the consideration of the Board of Directors. This innovation is to put the girl students on an equal footing with the boys by giving the girls something corresponding to Bar Mitzvah." Berman went on to assert that the "innovation" would make girls more serious and cognizant of their Jewish responsibilities.

catch on in Conservative synagogues nationally.* Local resistance, if any, was residual and faint. After the first bat mitzvah at Minneapolis's Beth El synagogue in 1948, one congregant recalls, Rabbi David Aronson peered out a window and said, "I don't see

*However, it was not until after World War II that even one-third of Conservative synagogues reported that they allowed the bat mitzvah ceremony.

Ellen Dinerstein reads from the Torah at Shir Tikvah Congregation, St. Paul, 1993. Beside her is Rabbi Stacy Offner.

any lightning. I don't hear any thunder." The heavens did not fall in 1949, either, when Beth El Women's League members read from the Torah on the bimah for the first time.

In a sense, however, time did stand still for the next two decades. While the Saturday-morning bat mitzvah ceremony became a staple at Conservative synagogues regionally, Jewish girls' mothers continued to play an extremely limited role in the religious services. It was not until the early 1970s, a time when the Reform movement began admitting women to the rabbinate and when Ezrat Nashim, a group of New York-based Jewish feminists, demanded gender equality in the Conservative movement, that change finally occurred. In the Upper Midwest rabbis soon included women in the minyan and allowed them equality in all aspects of the religious services.

In the 1970s, too, women stepped into new professional roles at the synagogue. Previously their purview had been limited to teaching Sunday school, but during these years they became administrators of synagogues and congregation presidents. In the 1980s women ascended to the pulpit as cantors and rabbis as well. In 1996 two Minnesota-born women were serving as rabbis for St. Paul congregations.

·

While immersion in the mikvah is an ancient religious obligation of women and thus an act of piety, it falls outside both the realms of domestic duty and synagogue attendance. Traditional Jewish women are supposed to immerse themselves in a pool of clear water before marriage and then after each menstrual period. They can have sexual intercourse only after visiting the mikvah. In large cities of the Upper Midwest, the mikvah is maintained by the community at large.* In the region's smaller towns, and especially on farms, women had to be more creative.

---

*The mikvah is used by men and women undergoing conversion to Judaism. Exceptionally pious men also visit the mikvah before Rosh Hashanah and Yom Kippur in order to purify themselves for the High Holidays. Some men even use the mikvah before the Sabbath.

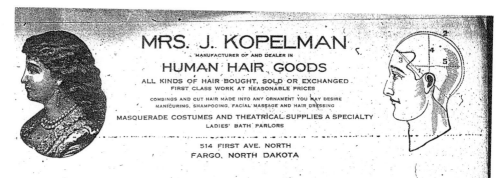

MRS. J. KOPELMAN
MANUFACTURER OF AND DEALER IN
HUMAN HAIR GOODS
ALL KINDS OF HAIR BOUGHT, SOLD OR EXCHANGED
FIRST CLASS WORK AT REASONABLE PRICES

COMBINGS AND CUT HAIR MADE INTO ANY ORNAMENT YOU MAY DESIRE
MANICURING, SHAMPOOING, FACIAL MASSAGE AND HAIR DRESSING

MASQUERADE COSTUMES AND THEATRICAL SUPPLIES A SPECIALTY
LADIES' BATH PARLORS

514 FIRST AVE. NORTH
FARGO, NORTH DAKOTA

Feb. 6, 1912.

AGREEMENT TO MAKING "MIKVAY".

MRS. J. KOPELMAN*********FARGO HEBREW CONGREGATION.

1st....That a plunge bath be made in Mrs. J. Kopelman's building--512 1st Ave. No., Fargo, N. D.

2nd....That every Hebrew women of Fargo, pay Mrs. J. Kopelman, the sum of $1.00, for every time they use said plunge bath, and that Mrs. J. Kopelman furnish towels, water, and soap. *also bath.*

3rd....That said plunge bath, (known as "MIKVAY"), be governed under the above and following agreements, as long as the said building is in Mrs. J. Kopel'man's possession, and that should Mrs. J. Kopelman rent out the building, 512-1st Ave., N., Fargo, or move out or for some other *reason* lose possession of, of said building, or sell same, she will have to refund money to Fargo Hebrew Congregation, in the sum of $130, but should said plunge bath be destroyed by fire, Mrs. J. Kopelman, will not stand any responsibility whatsoever.

4th....That should the Fargo Hebrew Congregation, not want to use the said "Mikvay", Mrs. J. Kopelman, will be sole owner of same, and the Fargo Hebrew Congregation will have nothing to do with same, other than use it, under aforesaid conditions.

Pres. *M. Levity*)
Vice Pres. *J. Salazy*) Representtitives of
Sec. *Jos. L. Shalit*) Fargo Hebrew Congregation.

_____

Owner of building.

The mikvah agreement between Lena Kopelman and the Fargo Hebrew Congregation

During the 1870s pioneer Eastern European women in St. Paul were said to have used Gervais Lake, north of town. Sophie Turnoy Trupin's father built a mikvah for his wife on their North Dakota farm early in this century. The windmill pumped water into a cement-lined miniature swimming pool that was enclosed in a wooden structure. During the same period one or two other farm families had mikvahs, and wives also used Painted Woods Creek, according to Joe Dokovna's recollections of Jewish farming couples in central North Dakota. Fargo, North Dakota, had a mikvah in the basement of a commercial establishment in the early twentieth century. The one in Aberdeen, South Dakota, dating from about 1920, was situated in the basement of a private home. There is some indication that Jewish women used the Finnish bathhouse in Virginia, Minnesota, as an informal substitute. Doubtless there were other mikvahs regionally that have eluded the historical record.

By the 1920s the mikvah was generally ignored by both Reform and Conservative women and even by many Orthodox women. They cast off the ritual, calling it oppressive and a stigma on women. Recently, however, this women's space has undergone reevaluation and revitalization. One reason for the upsurge in mikvah use is the growth of the Lubavich Hassidim—a fundamentalist strain within Orthodox Judaism that is characterized by close-knit group cohesion and an acceptance of charismatic leadership. Although centered in New York City, the movement runs a national school for women, the Bais Chanah, in St. Paul and has enough adherents to fill synagogues in both St. Paul and Minneapolis. The Jewish women's movement has also found new meaning in the ablution ceremony. Its adherents view the mikvah as an autonomous space for women, and the waters are perceived as an aid to spiritual and psychic cleansing.

Like all traditionally oriented European Jewish women, Sarah Balkind wore a sheitel (wig).

VOICES

WORSHIP AT HOME

Dorothy Mosow Hurwitz recalled her grandmother praying in her family's Sioux City, Iowa, home in the 1920s.

Oh yes, my grandmother davened [prayed] every morning and every evening. . . . In the bedroom generally where she wouldn't disturb anyone else.

———

Daisy Ginsburg Mains was born in 1891 on St. Paul's West Side. Her parents and grandmother emigrated from Russia in 1881.

My mother's mother Sarah Balkind lived with us until she died when I was fourteen years old. . . . She wore a full length skirt and a gathered apron, very full and with huge pockets. In those pockets she always had some pennies and candy. She rewarded us with either which was a great treat. She wore a "shetle" (a wig, the orthodox custom). I never saw her without it. She taught us our morning and evening prayers in Hebrew. She played cards with us. She fed us far beyond our needs.

WORSHIP ON THE FARM

Celia Kamins's family farmed in North Dakota beginning about 1912.

There were about 35 Jewish families in the entire settlement that went from Regan to Rhame, [North Dakota] . . . and back to our place. . . . The farmers would all come for the holidays. We had one or two men who . . . were religious men, and they would conduct services for the holidays. The women all brought their food, enough for what they knew their families would need for the two or three days. We slept on the floor in the dining room:

The tables and chairs were carried out. We filled the ticks with straw and spread them on the floor. The beds that we had were used by the men. . . . But it was figured that way because they felt that the women would get up in the morning and clear the ticks away so that we could set up the tables and chairs to serve breakfast. . . . [T]he men would milk the cows and feed the horses and chickens [and] take care of everything while the women had all this work to do in the house. They had their breakfast and then services would begin. And then around noon, the women would go out into the kitchen, prepare lunch and serve it to everyone.

————

Sophie Turnoy Trupin's family farmed near Wilton, North Dakota, about 1910.

[O]n the day preceding *Yom Kippur* all the Jewish homesteaders, who were scattered over many miles, gathered their families and started on a journey to a common meeting place in order to observe the holiest day of the year. The farmhouse that could accommodate the most worshippers was the house of the Weinbergs. It was to be our *shul* [synagogue]. . . .

The scene that night in the improvised synagogue is still with me. . . . Each woman had lit the ritual candle for her own family in the living room downstairs, and all about on tables and chests stood the flickering candles. As soon as the men had put up their horses and unloaded provisions, they went upstairs, draped themselves in prayer shawls, and commenced to pray. The women took care of the household chores and then joined the worshippers at the other end of the room. . . . They found it sweet to hear the old tunes and to be surrounded by their own people. They prayed with the fervor of those who have been deprived of something they had always taken for granted.

WORSHIP IN SMALL TOWNS

Rita Pomerance Gusack's parents first taught school near Lehr, North Dakota. Other relatives farmed nearby.

The synagogue and congregation of Wishek, North Dakota, about 1920

My parents were married in late October, 1912. Because there was no Synagogue or Rabbi, they had to wait and set their wedding date to coincide with the time that the traveling Rabbi from Minnesota came, and he came in October of that year for he had a lot of babies to circumcise. . . . When the High Holidays would come every one that could would go to Bismarck and stay with friends or relatives. But by 1913 there was a big enough group . . . to start a small Synagogue in Ashley. . . . My mother remembers that the Synagogue was set up in an old house, but she does not remember how often the Rabbi came for services.

———

Myer Shark's family owned a clothing store in Devils Lake, North Dakota. The location for religious services he described is surely a singular one.

It was a practice of the County Commissioners and the District Judge to arrange the terms of Court and the trials so that at no time was a date ever set [during] the fall of the year until they first checked with one of the Jewish men in town [to find out] when the Jewish holidays fell. . . . The congregation had a cabinet built in which was kept the Torah scrolls. . . . [It was] moved into the Courtroom the day before the holiday [started when] the congregation put their own padlock on the swinging doors, and they carried the key from that time until the close of the Yom Kippur service about ten days later. . . . [At home] I picked up the gleaming white tablecloths that my mother had set aside . . . and I took them up to the Courtroom so that they could be spread on all of the tables and on the podium [and] the Judge's bench. . . . [For services,] there was a rabbi present [and] attendance would be about 65 people [who] lived in Devils Lake [and came] also from many of the smaller towns around [such as] Lakota, Maddock, and Rugby. . . . [T]he start of it was in about 1918 or 1920, and the arrangement ended in 1938 or 1939. . . . [I]t was highly unusual and indicative of a nice [sort of] inter-religious feeling that existed in the community.

————

Emily Zvorist Rodd's family owned a grocery store in Bismarck, North Dakota, in the 1920s.

[T]here were quite a few of the Jewish people who came to Bismarck from the small towns for the holidays, and I remember very well the big holiday celebrations in a rented hall—and the delicious wines, and breads, fruits . . . that were a part of the holidays—and after the services at the hall all of the people that had come in from the neighboring towns would be invited to someones [*sic*] house—and our house was always overflowing—my mother was a wonderful cook, and everyone wanted to come to have her chicken soup.

WOMEN'S PRAYER AND PLACE IN SYNAGOGUES

Rose Feldman Straus was born in Latvia and arrived in Minot, North Dakota, in 1906.

And in our synagogue in the old country there was a balcony completely shut off from the men, and that is where the women sat. Well here they couldn't afford such a thing, and after all we were a little more modern than that, and the women sat on one side and the men on the other, the women sat sort of toward the back, but not together. . . . But you see the old-timers, they're all gone. . . . The younger people, who are now the old-timers, we do what we want to do, and there's no one to say, "No, you mustn't do that." We do it just the way we think. . . . And men and women, nobody would think of going to the synagogue, and the wife sitting on one side and the man on the other.

————

Ruth Firestone married Howard Brin in 1941. They lived in Minneapolis after Brin's discharge from the armed services at the end of World War II.

[I]n about 1953, when Rabbi Rabinowitz came to the Adath Jeshurun [synagogue] he, knowing that I was a poet, asked me to write material that could be used as supplementary material in services. That got me involved in a very long career, if you want to use that word, which I've pursued for probably thirty years, which was writing new liturgy . . . that could be acceptable to modern people and meaningful . . . to women. As I was writing, the Jewish feminist movement began to emerge, and it coincided with my ideas and feelings.

————

Nadia Ackerman Smirnov emigrated from the Soviet Union to St. Paul in 1989. Her daughter, Masha, became a bat mitzvah in 1991.

You see, when I go to the Temple [of Aaron], I don't understand any words. I like this music, I enjoy the atmosphere, and I
feel Jewish at that time—I really feel it. But I take this [prayer
book], and I don't understand anything. . . . I've seen other people who understand, and my Masha now understands. And it is
very important for her. I am glad that she has now this feeling and
she can express more than me. . . . We don't realize it sometimes,
but through our children, our kids, we are closer, and it's not an
easy process for us, because [in the Soviet Union] we didn't have
an opportunity to study, we didn't have an opportunity to think
about it. . . . If somebody told me three years ago in the Soviet
Union my Masha is going to have [a] Bat Mitzvah [I wouldn't
have believed them].

————

*Carol Porter Berlin was raised in Minot, North Dakota. In the
1980s she and her husband joined Adas Israel in St. Paul, a synagogue attended by many adherents of the Lubavich Hasidim.*

I like the way it is so casual and people come in with their
strollers, and people are talking here, and people are *davening*
[praying] there. . . . It's not hard to be behind the *mekhitzah**
because I was developing intense friendships with the women,
and I was drinking the whole thing in.
    One thing . . . that I liked immediately about the lifestyle is
that it takes place inside the home and inside the family life and
not only in the *shul* [synagogue]. So I feel that my not having a
huge relationship with the *shul* really doesn't matter, and I am
equally a part of the community as anybody else.

WOMEN'S SYNAGOGUE-BASED TEACHING
EFFORTS AND ORGANIZATIONS

*Jeannette L. Agrant grew up in Sioux Falls, South Dakota, dur-
ing the first decade of this century. Her home was an outpost of*

*The *mekhitza* is the divider, either a screen or partial wall, which separates
men from women in the synagogue.

Jewish culture. The home services she described were held about 1904.

I attended social gatherings at the Methodist Church until asked to become a member. My father said, "that is enough." We had little religious training and no congregation at the time. Services for the High Holidays were held in our home. We had a Torah and a shofar [a trumpet made from a ram's horn], and an elderly uncle led services. . . . [M]y sister Sarah and I started the first religious class for children [about 1919].

––––––––

Florence Silberstein Gidding's parents were early settlers in Duluth.

The actual beginnings of our Sunday School in Duluth, as nearly as I can remember, came about indirectly through Dickens' Christmas Carol. In about 1892, or 1893, Mrs. Fannie Mondshine's sister, Ray Rosenblat, . . . adapted the Christmas Carol for use as a Jewish play, which a group of eager Jewish children happily enacted. . . . This interest in Jewish activity spurred us on to organize the Sunday School. As there had been no organized Jewish juvenile education at all, the idea met with the whole community's hearty approval. . . . Of course we had to hold the school meetings in whatever available hall we could get. . . . Following our lead, the parents decided to organize a congregation in earnest.

––––––––

Edith Guttman Mesonznick recalled religious life in Aberdeen, South Dakota, during the late 1940s and the 1950s.

In between rabbis I taught Sunday School and Hebrew School in the synagogue. Perhaps, because we were so far away . . . we felt the need to be more "religious" about our observances of our religion. All of us attended the various holiday rites and celebrations and observed them for ourselves and our children.

More important, we were drawn together as one family, in spite of the different [groups] of Judaism[:] Orthodox, Conservative and Reform. I found this aspect of religion in Aberdeen to be very inspiring and continually marvelled at it. There was, of course, some quibbling among different members because of small differences in observation, but it was very minor and very amusing.

———————

The Deutsch family moved to Minneapolis in 1873. Marlchen Deutsch was a founding member of the Baszion Benevolent Society, which served the needs of Shaari Tof (Temple Israel).

In order to build a fence around this plot of ground [the cemetery], so that the cows would not eat the geraniums, the Ladies Benevolent Society gave a charity ball, at which sixty dollars was raised, with which was erected a wooden fence. The ball was attended by Jew and Gentile alike.

———————

Rochele Gela Mann recalled the efforts of the Fargo, North Dakota, Hebrew Ladies Aid Society—what she called the Jewish Women's Aid Society—at the turn of the century.

A Jewish Women's Aid Society was formed. They met in each others' homes. Their aims were to assist Jews who were in need of financial assistance or loans for a horse, money to buy goods to peddle, to start a new business etc. This was all done with no interest charged.

A converted Jewess from Sweden was the secretary of the society. . . . Mrs. Ackerman brought [to] the attention [of] the society that they were in need of a Sunday School for Jewish education of the children. A teacher was hired. Being in need of a place to learn, this caused a collection of monies and a synagogue was built. Then a library was needed so the society gave two Sholom

Aleichem plays. After the first play was given in a local theatre, the gentile community loved it and asked that they repeat a second play. Bibles and books were then purchased. Mother[,] who was 4 months pregnant with me, was teased as she acted out her role in the plays.

―――――――

The following tragic case, recorded in the minutes of the Fargo Hebrew Ladies Aid Society, from 1921 to 1928, indicated the limited capacity of the society and the reluctance of its members to take the final step.

Sister Hartstein reported that Mrs. Cohen* is in trouble with her husband, And Sister Siegel was to go and investigate about the case. [Apparently the husband had deserted the family because he is not mentioned again.] Sister reported that Mrs. Cohen is settled down in a flat, and has the children with her, the Sisters should make it a rule to go and visit her if things are not clear that the children are not kept clean to see that she keeps them clean, but not to help her. . . . Made a motion by B. Hartstein and second by Kirsel to investigate Mrs. Cohen if she is in need of Aid. . . . Made motions and second that $23.00 for Cohen's for board and room. . . . It was moved and second[ed] that all necessary things should be bought for the little children of Sarah Cohen. . . . A report was made by . . . sister Molly Shapiro that Sarah Cohen is in the County Hospital and in rather nervous condition . . . that Sarah Cohen was in a critical condition. . . . Sister Tillie Siegel . . . told us how Sarah Cohen was getting along. Then she asked the Ladies Aid Society to help dress up her two little children. Motion made by Sister Tillie Naftalin and seconded by Sister Shapiro that the Ladies Aid shall allow amount needed for dressing up these two children. . . . A complaint was brought in that Sarah Cohen's children are without warm clothing. It was moved and seconded

*The woman's name has been changed.

that sister Molly Shapiro shall investigate and see what is needed, motion carried and to buy what is most necessary. . . . Each and every member were very glad to know that Sarah Cohen's children are already in a home. Lets [sic] all hope that they will have a good home. . . . Money paid out $45.64 for dressing up the Cohen children before they left for the Cleveland home [a national Jewish orphanage]. . . . Mrs. Tillie Siegel finally found a home for Sarah with a woman by name Mrs. Johnson who is trying very hard to do all she can for Sarah, but Mrs. Johnson has reported that she does not wish to care for Sarah any longer. And if this is so Sarah will have to be sent to Jamestown Hospital [a state mental institution], this being the last resort. Mrs. Siegel wishes to make this clear to all members that was not her that will send Sarah to Jamestown. That she has done everything she can do in finding Sarah a home. . . . Mrs. Tillie Siegel gave the report of her work[;] she also read a letter from the Superintendant of Jamestown hospital stating that . . . Sarah Cohen is not doing so very well.

Winnie Lewis Roth's eulogy for Etta Silk Hallock, who was president of her synagogue's women's auxiliary during the early decades of the century, summarizes the kinds of activities pursued by any ladies' aid society, whether Jewish or non-Jewish.

When Eli S. Woolfan purchased an old Finnish Church in North Hibbing [for use as a synagogue] the work of the Sisters of Peace really commenced. The women took on the job of furnishing the kitchen. . . . Etta was duly elected president, and in those days campaigns were spirited, and more than one presidential candidate went out for office—and sometimes, I am told, the defeated candidate got mad and quit. . . . The society conducted booths at the County Fair, held public dinners and dances, and raised significant sums—the hard way. . . . [Etta] acted as an unofficial social worker and employment service, too, when there was need for that type of help.

———

The August 1946 St. Paul Temple of Aaron Women's League minutes reveal two functions of that group's program—synagogue beautification and the promotion of interfaith understanding.

"The Jewish Home Beautiful" will [be] feature[d at] our first meeting of the year. . . . All church groups in the vicinity are to be invited. Each neighbor may also bring a gentile neighbor or guest.

———

Dorothy Mosow Hurwitz explained the work entailed in preparing for the Harvest Festival of Mount Zion Temple of Sioux Falls, South Dakota. It was held annually during the 1960s and early 1970s.

We used to have a bazaar and a dinner where we served the non-Jewish community, anywhere from 700 to 800 people, this handful of Jewish women. We served matzoh ball soup. We used to make *farfel* [a type of noodle] casseroles and meat rolled in cabbage—*prackas,* and mostly traditional food. We'd have some chickens or something and then pastries, and we used to sell all this food, package it, sell it. We made all our own bread, bagel[s], coffee cakes. I spent more time at the Temple than I did at home for many years.

THE MIKVAH

Frances Kaufman Milavetz lived in Virginia, Minnesota, and was married in about 1935.

Before I was married my mother . . . told me that when I got married she wanted me to go to [the] Mikvah. Although I did not think it was a wonderful idea, I went for her sake.

———

Rabbi Elka Abrahamson grew up in St. Paul. Since 1993, she and her husband, Rabbi Martin Zinkow, have served St. Paul's Mount Zion Congregation.

The St. Paul mikvah, early 1990s

Mikvah is very big now for all kind[s] of rituals for women[,] whereas [it] was scorned twenty five or thirty years ago as an oppressive ritual. It is now being celebrated as a cleansing ritual. . . . One woman who struggled with infertility issues . . . used [the] mikvah to signify an end to the struggle with her own body.

THE RABBI

Julie Gordon grew up in Albert Lea, Minnesota, during the 1960s and early 1970s. She and her husband, Jonathan Ginsburg, began serving jointly as rabbis of St. Paul's Temple of Aaron in 1988.

It was hard [being the only Jew in my public school class,] but what helped me [to] create my Jewish identity was Herzl Camp [a Zionist/religious camp]. . . . Later I got very involved in USY [United Synagogue Youth, the national youth organization of the Conservative movement]. [Still l]ater I started a chapter in Albert Lea. . . .

Well I would come up [to the Twin Cities] especially in my junior and senior year[s] almost every other Shabbat. . . . The Twin Cities became my Jewish community. . . .

I really wanted to have a Bat Mitzvah . . . so finally at fifteen, I kept nudging and nudging my parents. . . . They said, "We're not religious. If Bert Cooper's daughters don't need a Bat Mitzvah, why do you need it?"* Then they finally said, "Well, if you can get any other girls to do it with you, then it would be OK.". . . So I got Andrea and Julie Seltzer. . . . Andrea was 17, I was 16, Julie was 15. . . . Bert taught us. . . . We were triple *B'not Mitzvah* in the basement of my house. . . . In fact we didn't have an *Aron Hakodesh* [literally, Holy Ark: a special receptacle where the Torah is kept], so Esther Seltzer had a beautiful armoire that we had to move from her house to our house so we had an appropriate place for the Torah. . . . We split the Haftorah [prophetic reading] into thirds. I don't know if I read from the Torah. My cousin, Jeff Gordon . . . read the Torah, [and] tons of my friends from USY, from all over the Midwest came and we had Shabbat in Albert Lea.

————

Rabbis Elka Abrahamson and Martin Zinkow of St. Paul's Mount Zion Congregation are the parents of four children.

I can't say that women bring any one thing to their pulpits except for being women, which I think is a powerful statement for Judaism—that women are on the *bimah*, they are in the boardrooms, they are reading Torah, they are taking their own learning seriously. . . . I am not sure you would find any one quality that runs across every female rabbi. . . . I think that as women, there has been a transformation that has taken place. I don't know that it has taken place within Judaism, but [rather] for individual Jews and for individual synagogues . . . and communities.

*Bert Cooper led services and taught children in the Austin-Albert Lea vicinity for decades until his death in 1995.

One Purim a fourth grader in my congregation wanted to dress up as a rabbi.* Her mother went out and bought her a black coat and hat and *payes* [side locks] and a beard. She looked at her mother and said, "I'm Rabbi Abrahamson. I'm going to wear a suit [skirt and jacket]." . . . She [also] wore a *tallit* [prayer shawl], had a pacifier pinned to her collar and had a baby in a [Snugli].

*Purim, like Halloween, involves masquerades, especially for children.

CHAPTER SIX

"Always Involved with Some Organization"
Women and Organizations

[M]y earliest memories involve my grandmother Pertzik . . . and she was always involved with some organization . . . whether it was the St. Paul Talmud Torah, the Women's Free Loan Association . . . , the Hakhnoses Orkhim, [or] the West Side Cemetery Association. [S]he used to go around from door to door . . . collecting money to help those who were . . . in need. . . . If you opened the drawer in the dining room, it was full of about twenty pushkes *[collection boxes] for organizations in New York or Palestine. . . . And this, from a woman who was widowed in 1927 with a houseful of children and no visible means of support.*

MARVIN PERTZIK'S 1980s recollections of his grandmother's *pushkes* and her devotion to the causes they represented are not unusual. Her actions potently symbolized a deep-seated religious obligation to perform tzedakah (righteous deeds). The pennies, nickels, and dimes his grandmother and other Jewish women individually dropped in their *pushkes* supported yeshivas, orphanages, and old-age homes in the United States, Europe, and Palestine.

But Jewish women in the Upper Midwest and America at large also devoted themselves to organizational auxiliaries—of Talmud Torahs, hospitals, and the many other charitable and philanthropic institutions that are essential to the local, national, and international Jewish community. The creation of these newer, non-synagogue-related auxiliaries began in the Upper Midwest around the turn of the century.

At about the same time, women also started forming organizations, such as the National Council of Jewish Women (NCJW) and Hadassah, that were not structurally affiliated with, or beholden to, any male-dominated association or institution. The idea of this kind of independence found willing listeners in the Upper Midwest. One of them was Sarah Lewis, of Chisholm, Minnesota. On a visit to Madison, Wisconsin, in 1919 she heard Hadassah founder Henrietta Szold speak and was so impressed that she founded a chapter of the organization as soon as she returned home. According to her daughter, Rhana Lewis Greenberg, Szold's oratory led Sarah to become "a convert to Zionism," and many other women were "*farbrente* (zealous) Hadassah ladies too."

•

Jewish-American women have typically joined organizations in large numbers and generally have been active on behalf of more than one cause. And their causes have been multitudinous. A 1920 issue of the Twin Cities newspaper *American Jewish World* listed twenty-six women's organizations in Minneapolis and ten in St. Paul—for a Jewish population that then totaled about twenty-five thousand.

These numbers reflected a world view: Jewish women were raised to feel it part of their responsibility to support causes outside their own homes and neighborhoods. High levels of community involvement continued through the decades. For example, a 1958 survey

An early-twentieth-century *pushke* (collection box). Money deposited in this box went to various charitable and religious institutions in Jerusalem. Customarily, women put money into *pushkes* before the Sabbath.

of the Minneapolis Jewish community reported that 81 percent of women had Jewish organizational affiliations: Within that group, 48 percent belonged to either one or two groups, and 52 percent belonged to three or more. During the decades of heavy immigration and on through the 1960s, Jewish women saw social needs all around them, and they became *farbrente* in support of their particular causes.

The plethora of organizations was a sign as well that the Jewish community was hardly monolithic. Before World War II, a vast cultural, political, philosophical, religious, and economic gulf separated German and Eastern European Jews. The latter group was itself splintered into religious, socialist, and Zionist interest groups, each of which spawned numerous subgroups. Historically, membership in the NCJW was drawn from the German-Jewish community, while Zionist causes always received greater support from Eastern European Jews and their descendants. Eastern European-rooted organizations practiced a high degree of mutual aid. Those created by German-Jewish women were designed to aid but also Americanize the immigrant.

The first organizations founded by Jewish women from Eastern Europe were similar to *khevres*. As members of the Bikur Kholim society, they visited the sick and brought kosher food to the hospitalized. They cared for the traveler at the Hakhnoses Orkhim (rest stop for the wayfarer). They supported religious education in America by forming auxiliaries to the Talmud Torahs that met after school and on weekends.

They also loaned each other money. The Charity Loan Society of St. Paul was founded by women in 1890. While no records of this society have survived, evidence does exist about the Women's Free Loan Society. Begun in about 1915 by Zlota Rivka Svidelsky, who lived on the West Side, it was run by and for women. Here a newly arrived immigrant could secure a loan in order to furnish a home or start a business. Unlike many St. Paul men's loan societies, this group charged no interest.

Although the loan society, Bikur Kholim, and Hakhnoses Orkhim disappeared, generally by the 1960s, there were at all times func-

The women's auxiliary that supported the St. Paul Hebrew Institute, about 1918. The institute was located on the city's West Side.

tioning social-welfare organizations through which Upper Midwestern Jewish women could direct their efforts. They, like women from other ethnic groups and many non-Jewish middle-class American women, put their time and energies into supporting facilities for the ill and aged. In the interwar period, for example, the Daughters of Abraham in St. Paul and the Ladies' Hebrew Hospital Society in Minneapolis worked to create a kosher facility for ailing Jewish people. Despite their best fund-raising efforts, it was not until after World War II that the St. Paul group was able to create a facility for Jews who were chronically ill. (At that time, the Jewish Home for the Aged, in St. Paul, would only admit healthy elderly people.) The new facility was named the Sholom Residence. Of course, it had its own active auxiliary and corps of volunteers.

Perhaps the most successful Jewish women's auxiliary in the Twin Cities was that of Mount Sinai Hospital. Founded by a group of Minneapolis Jewish businessmen, the hospital opened its doors in 1950. This was a particularly significant development because, for some decades, Jewish physicians had been refused hospital-admitting privileges in Minneapolis. The Mount Sinai auxiliary, whose mission was to provide funds, volunteers, and help with public relations, was an immediate success. There were sixteen hundred charter members and a peak membership, in 1965, of twenty-six hundred. It was the largest Jewish women's organization, as well as the largest hospital auxiliary, in Minneapolis. Members worked in the wards, in the laundry and pharmacy, and ran the coffee and gift shops. They conducted annual book fairs and balls with flair and raised substantial sums. Regardless of their diligence and accomplishments, women had no vote on the hospital's board of governors until 1973. While Mount Sinai Hospital itself closed in the early 1990s, a trust set up by the auxiliary continues to fund medical and educational needs in the Twin Cities Jewish community.

The Jewish Home for the Aged, an outgrowth of the Charity Loan Society described above, as well as the Sisters of Peace Benevolent Society, was founded in 1906. Two years later the

The Mount Sinai Hospital Auxiliary raised significant sums between the mid-1950s and the early 1990s, when the hospital closed.

group, now numbering 220 women, had collected enough funds to buy a facility and install eight "inmates," as residents were then called. As the need for funds increased, Home for the Aged president Mary Burton persuaded a group of men to take control of the board of directors. Once they did, she became vice-president. But by 1909, the board was entirely male. The women then formed an auxiliary that blurred the line between philanthropy and client intake: Some of its members actually made decisions about admissions. Fund-raising, however, was the auxiliary's primary goal. During the 1920s, for instance, the organization's annual Purim Ball was among the local Jewish community's main social events. Through various structural splits and recombinations, the auxil-

Groundbreaking for a new Sholom Home building, St. Paul, late 1970s. Ada Rubenstein (right) was the first female president of the institution's board of directors in more than sixty years.

iary continued to be a financial mainstay of the Jewish Home for the Aged. In 1971 the boards and auxiliaries of the Home for the Aged and Sholom Residence merged, and a new entity, Sholom Home, Inc., was established. The first head of the combined auxiliary, Ada Rubenstein, went on in the late 1970s to become president of the institution's board of directors. She was the first woman to lead the board since Mary Burton. In 1996 Sholom Home auxiliary membership exceeded thirty-seven hundred. A yearly ball was still the principal fund-raiser, although it was no longer held at Purim.

A new form of auxiliary developed after World War II, one that has gained a great deal of strength in the Upper Midwest, and nationally, since the 1960s: the women's "division" (or subsidiary) of the Jewish Federation, an umbrella organization functioning in each Jewish community whose purposes are similar to those of the United Way or Community Chest. The federations raise and allocate funds for Jewish social-service, cultural, and educational activities locally as well as nationally and internationally. The federations have been collectively described by some social scientists as the preeminent institution in American Jewish life, both because of the wide-ranging nature of the tasks they perform and because of their ability to bridge intra-religious differences in pursuit of community-building. The importance and prestige of the work lead hundreds of women voluntarily to attend federation-organized educational, motivational, and leadership-training sessions before soliciting funds for a spectrum of Jewish causes. The status of the federations allows them to choose proven community leaders to head campaigns and to train young leaders.

But positions as federation leaders have not come to women easily. Operating chiefly through the women's divisions, they long had only minimal representation on male-dominated federation boards of directors. It was not until the mid-1970s that they began to be elected presidents of Upper Midwestern federation boards. Their status on these boards is still evolving, for some professional women resent being placed in a women's division rather than in a gender-neutral category.

In the late 1940s and early 1950s, the women's division of the Minneapolis Federation for Jewish Service annually conducted comprehensive one-day fund-raising campaigns. Since that time, the federation's fund-raising has grown lengthier and more sophisticated.

Independent Jewish women's organizations, characteristically, follow the model of American women's clubs. These organizations tend to have a nationwide membership and a bureaucracy composed of both volunteers and paid workers. Typically, programs and fund-raising quotas are developed at the national level and presented to the local units for implementation. Programs generally carry some emotional appeal to women's maternal or Zionist concerns.

The oldest of these independent groups is the National Council of Jewish Women (NCJW), which was founded in 1893; in 1996 it had a national membership of about one hundred thousand. Nina Morais Cohen of Minneapolis and Rachel Haas of St. Paul attended its birth, at the Chicago World's Fair Council of Religions. The two women set up Minneapolis and St. Paul units, called sections, soon after their return to the Twin Cities. Duluth's NCJW section was founded about twenty years later. The organization appealed mainly to women in the Reform movement, offering them opportunities for both study and social action—as attested by the motto, "Faith and Humanity." The deepening of faith, in the form of Bible study, was the first undertaking of the fledgling group. Rabbi Emanuel Hess, of St. Paul's Mount Zion Congregation, led the group, which was made up primarily of that congregation's women. Nina Morais Cohen herself headed the Minneapolis study group. She was a formidable scholar, and her class syllabi were adopted by NCJW sections around the country.

The NCJW established a tradition of providing its members with stimulating educational opportunities. After World War II, for example, many study groups were led by the University of Minnesota professors who developed courses similar to ones that were later offered through the school's Continuing Education for Women program. Course offerings proliferated through the 1950s. While the NCJW still presents educational programs, they are not so intensive as in the past. In addition, they face considerable competition from those organized by other cultural and educational institutions.

It was in the area of social action, however, that the NCJW truly left its mark. At the turn of the century it aided the Eastern European Jews who were then streaming into the country. The needs of Jewish children and mothers were the chief concern of Upper Midwestern NCJW sections. Early in the century, the Minneapolis section appointed one of its members to assist Jewish children brought before juvenile courts. Both Twin Cities sections founded settlement houses. Neighborhood House, on St. Paul's West Side, had its beginnings in 1897 as the NCJW Industrial School. The St. Paul section also helped establish the Capitol Community Center, and the Minneapolis section founded the South Side Settlement House, in 1932, in an area populated by Rumanian Jews. The NCJW also set up, staffed, and paid for fresh-air camps, nursery schools, Sabbath schools, and literary societies.

After World War II, the NCJW focused its social-service programs mainly on the needs of the aged and children. The Minneapolis section, for example, created a social and recreational program for elderly Jews at the Emanuel Cohen Center on the city's North Side in 1947. Five years later it funded the Council House for Senior Citizens, which provided the entire city's elderly population with a drop-in center that offered educational, cultural, and recreational activities. The St. Paul section followed suit in 1961 by creating the Leisure League cultural and educational program for senior citizens at the Jewish Community Center.

In the 1960s both Twin Cities NCJW sections instituted substantial volunteer projects in the public schools. The St. Paul section started an early-childhood school-preparedness program, which in 1967 was taken over by the federally funded Head Start program. Later, it offered supplemental reading instruction in the schools. The Minneapolis section ran similar programs, first offering after-school, then, in the mid-1960s, in-school tutoring. To maintain a healthy number of volunteer tutors, the section capped its service to the Minneapolis school system by bringing together, in 1967, a coalition of Jewish and non-Jewish women's groups to form Women in Service to Education.

When the Soviet Union began allowing Jews to emigrate in the early 1970s, the NCJW responded with initiatives to aid the immigrants, such as one-on-one language instruction and programs that paired American families with newly arrived Russians in order to provide American mentors and spark intercultural friendships. Through activities of this kind, the NCJW has, in a sense, returned to its early social-service roots—but with a more personal emphasis.

During the last three decades, as more and more women have joined the work force, the NCJW has shifted from large-scale social-service projects, each involving many volunteers, to particularized advocacy and lobbying efforts. For these activities the NCJW often works in conjunction with other similar women's organizations on issues typically involving the well-being of women and children, the aged, and the ailing.

America's second-oldest independent women's organization is Hadassah. Founded by scholar and educator Henrietta Szold in New York City in 1912, it claimed in the mid-1990s a national membership of 370,000. Hadassah draws both on the ideology of Zionism and on women's sense of social responsibility to make its members zealous in support of Israel's hospitals, youth activities, and educational services. Members also support the Jewish National Fund (JNF) by filling the modern blue-and-white *pushkes* with money.*

Numerous Hadassah chapters operate in the Upper Midwest. In 1996 regional membership stood at about thirty-five hundred.

The NCJW implemented numerous public school programs during the 1960s. This one, in 1967, provided supplementary education at St. Paul's McKinley elementary school.

*The JNF was founded in order to collect funds to buy land in Palestine from Arab owners. Later, the money financed swamp drainage and forest development. Presently, the JNF supports ecological projects.

Mrs. George Stillman (left), Mrs. Edward H. Sokol, and Mrs. Marshall Beaubaire look over plans for a new hospital and medical school in Palestine, 1946.

The Hadassah Tea Shoppe operated in the heart of downtown Minneapolis before World War II.

National programs that were implemented in the region from the 1920s to the 1940s included "linen showers," in which bedding, towels, and robes were donated, collected, and shipped to Hadassah medical units in Palestine. Milk bottles served as banks; the money in them went to support school-lunch programs in Palestine. The fund-raising intensified as, in 1936, the organization began planning a medical center in Jerusalem to be jointly run by Hadassah and Hebrew University. Fund-raising grew during that same time when Hadassah took on the task of providing German-Jewish children with homes in Palestine.

Hadassah chapters in the Upper Midwest have consistently met the fund-raising quotas set by the national organization. For

During the 1950s the Minneapolis chapter of Hadassah, to which Mrs. Norman Perl (left) and Mrs. Joe Cohn belonged, sponsored the Funtennial, an annual fair that filled Minneapolis's large downtown armory.

example, in the 1930s, the Minneapolis chapter ran a "tea shoppe" that sold Jewish delicacies in the heart of the downtown. Every chapter in the region held rummage sales, probably from the 1920s to the 1960s. Prior to the mid-1950s, members were allowed to donate time or handiwork in lieu of cash. This was thoughtful as well as democratic, for a cash-only contribution policy might have proven too burdensome for poorer members. Beginning in the 1950s, larger chapters rose to the challenge of meeting their

monetary quotas by producing enormous events. For instance, the Minneapolis chapter packed the city's vast armory for its annual Funtennial fund-raiser and awarded grand prizes such as deep freezers, mink stoles, and automobiles. After World War II, women in smaller chapters around the Upper Midwest worked just as hard producing theatrical events, selling Jewish foods, and serving countless dinners.

Raising funds for Jewish needs has been the raison d'être of every Jewish women's organization, whether constituted as an auxiliary of a larger body or as an autonomous group. As suggested, however, that is not the only function these organizations have performed. In small towns, they play a critical role by tying local women into a regional network. In this respect, Hadassah has been particularly successful. Aberdeen, Sioux Falls, and Watertown in South Dakota; Fargo, Grand Forks, and Bismarck in North Dakota; Mankato, the Iron Range towns, the Brainerd area, Winona, Duluth, and the Twin Cities—all still have, or have had, Hadassah chapters. Newsletters, regional conventions, and visits by regional Hadassah presidents have helped keep members in small towns geographically and emotionally connected to a larger entity.

Jewish women's organizations in small towns play still another part—that of Jewish-community ambassadors to non-Jews. By serving Jewish delicacies at dinners open to the entire populace, explaining Jewish holidays to church groups, hosting interfaith events, and cooperating with non-Jewish women's groups, they help remind the mainly Christian towns in which they reside that America is a pluralistic society. They have been effective, too, in explaining Israel's needs.

Women's organizations also help their members nurture a secular Jewish identity. As early as 1930, Rose Rosenthal, a regional president of Hadassah, reflected this development in a speech she gave to the Duluth chapter. "Living in an age when religion is on the decline," she said, "it is up to us Jewish women to guarantee Judaism for all posterity. . . . The work of Hadassah in Palestine has anchored its members to J[u]daism." Since the 1930s, Zionism has of course become an even greater element of Jewish-American

Beatrice Premack (left) and Gail Pickus of the Aberdeen, South Dakota, Hadassah chapter, early 1990s. Through the years, this chapter has met all its fund-raising quotas.

identity; supporting institutions in Israel continues to give members of Hadassah, the federation, and NCJW a chance to show their zeal.

Voluntary organizations have imparted leadership skills, from Nina Morais Cohen's study group, which helped turn-of-the-century Minneapolis Jewish women learn to think and write critically, down to the leadership and motivational-training courses of the present day. The organizations gave women a chance to hone abilities that no one outside their families knew they possessed and to take on new social responsibilities. "A lot of women who became active in women's organizations loved the power it gave them," observed Rosalyn Baker, who became president of the Minneapolis Hadassah chapter in the late 1950s. "They had talents without a professional outlet. [It was a] chance to exercise leadership between 1945 and 1975, to be powerful and develop a real sense of self."

In addition to filling roles in Jewish organizations, Upper Midwestern Jewish women have served in civic, educational, social-service, philanthropic, cultural, and political associations around the region. Their sense of social responsibility transferred easily into the nonsectarian arena. Nina Morais Cohen was a founder of the Woman's Club of Minneapolis as well as of the NCJW. Jennie Levitt started auxiliaries in mental hospitals around Minnesota in the 1950s and served as president of the Mount Sinai Hospital Auxiliary. Fanny Fliegelman Brin, who was national president of the NCJW in the mid-1930s, was a founder, along with Carrie Chapman Catt, of the National Committee on the Cause and Cure of War. She worked on peace issues her entire adult life.*

Through all the aforementioned activities, Jewish women have expanded their traditional roles of homemaker and guardian of domestic religiosity. Their concern and skill at solving social problems first impelled them into the wider community around the turn of the century—a time when the home was seen as their proper sphere. Like their Christian counterparts, they described their social activism as domestic housekeeping writ large. In doing so, they redefined socially acceptable behavior for women while not challenging the gender roles of the times. Furthermore, their concerns for the welfare of women and children, for the aged and ailing, and for the immigrant—all became concerns of the Jewish community as a whole.

Yet Jewish women and their organizations have also been marginalized in the communities they served. Women's auxiliaries have often been treated offhandedly by the men who lead the organizations to which the auxiliaries are attached. They have been expected to work backstage or in the kitchen, typically appearing only for a brief thanks and then being dismissed. Until the early 1970s they were routinely denied voting privileges on the boards of the institutions they served, and it was not until later in that decade that they were able to attain leadership positions in the Upper Midwest's Jewish-community institutions.

---

*Brin capped her peace-activism career by being chosen an alternate member of the United States delegation to the 1945 conference in San Francisco at which the United Nations charter was written.

In the 1990s Jewish women's organizations, both in the Upper Midwest and nationally, find themselves at a critical juncture. Because many women now hold full-time jobs, groups can no longer rely on their members to staff book fairs, serve dinners, or even volunteer for long-term social-service projects. In the 1970s the Jewish women's movement called into question the entire rationale behind separate women's associations, calling them a "rear guard" and asserting that they were unresponsive to the needs of contemporary women.

Yet auxiliaries and independent women's groups alike continue to serve important functions besides fund-raising. When women work together in kitchens, the culture they share and transmit goes well beyond the trading of recipes. While they still function as a training ground for leaders, Jewish women's organizations are becoming increasingly aware that they have to make changes in order to hold on to the loyalty of their members, particularly of the younger women. They are also aware that the Jewish community will be the poorer if they fail.

VOICES

PUSHKES

Toba Marcowitz Geller's family lived in Halliday, North Dakota, during the 1910s and 1920s. The rabbi who made the rounds to their home and many others also served as a conduit for information about other Jews in the state and in the world beyond North Dakota.

On the Rabbi's first visit he left with us a small, locked, blue metal box with the white Star of David painted on one side. . . . Six months later when Rabbi Mintz made his regular return visit, he brought with him the key which opened the box. He carefully counted the money each time, gave my parents a signed receipt, and took the money with him, leaving the empty box with us to begin all over again saving our change for his next visit. The money he collected was not for himself, but for Jewish charitable institutions in the large cities . . . or for worthy causes in Palestine.

EARLY AUXILIARIES AND MUTUAL-AID SOCIETIES

Ida Balick, who lived on St. Paul's West Side early in the century, gave a clear picture of how the money raised by mutual-aid societies was used.

I remember when we moved here they had an organization in the Talmud Torah where everybody put so much in, like in a kitty, and anybody that wanted to borrow—poor people . . . they gave them a loan. . . . They were poor and they had to have their money for coal in the winter [and] for food, [or] to pay their taxes. . . . [T]hey paid it back, sure, they paid it back in dribbles of what they could, but they paid it back.

———

The women's auxiliary of St. Paul's Jewish Home for the Aged was started in about 1909, after men had taken control of the board of directors. Sylvia Feinstein Peilen was born in 1897 into a St. Paul family that was committed to helping elderly Jews.

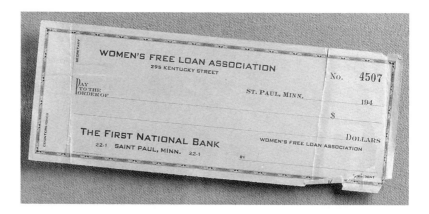

The Women's Free Loan Association was founded in St. Paul about 1915 to help newly arrived Jewish immigrants set up housekeeping.

[M]y mother, she was . . . one of several women who organized the first ladies' auxiliary of the Jewish Home for the Aged.
. . . During those years they had what is known as a Pound Party.
People would go out to certain members in the community to
collect food, and I remember getting a pound of coffee from this
one . . . and maybe a pound of sugar [from that one because]
people were not too wealthy and . . . the only way that the home
could [be] maintained was by collecting personal things from
people.

————

*At the turn of the century, women's auxiliaries that served
synagogues whose congregants were Eastern European Jews often
looked outward to fill unmet community needs. St. Paul's
Daughters of Abraham auxiliary (of the Sons of Abraham synagogue) was one such association during the 1920s, as Janet
Silberstein, the daughter of an active member, related.*

[The Daughters of Abraham's] first effort was seeking funds to
buy a hearse. . . then [they] began to save toward their kosher
"hospital." . . . Jennie Rosenthal held out her money-box to
everyone, after she would fasten the bit of bright ribbon to a
lapel. Take this money, from rummage, bake sales, teas, luncheons and dinners . . . from street collections, dues and memorials.
. . . [A] kosher home for the chronically ill had always been the
goal [and in] 1947 they . . . purchased a home . . . and named it
SHOLOM RESIDENCE.

————

*Ida Balick began her career as a volunteer by koshering chickens
and baking delicacies for the inhabitants of the Sholom Residence
during the early 1950s, when the facility was located in an old residence off St. Paul's Summit Avenue. A modern structure was built
in 1957. Some time after that, she became a cook. In an account
probably dating from the early 1960s, Balick gave her own ideas
about how to serve the patients' welfare.*

[Mr. Katz], he was ninety-some years old, . . . he says to me, "Mrs. Balick [I want] schmaltz herring," and he was on a salt free diet. . . . [I]f I'll ask [his doctor] he'll say, "No.". . . So [I said to a man who was] visiting his mother, "Ben, I want you to go to Cecil's [a St. Paul delicatessen] and get me a big fat herring with a big fat back." . . . I fixed the herring . . . and I boiled the potatoes. Well, if I would have given him . . . the best steak he wouldn't have been so thrilled . . . . [When his doctor] came to see him a couple of days later, [Mr. Katz] says, . . . "You don't know what Mrs. Balick did for me." So he told him. So [the doctor] comes to the kitchen and says, "I got to talk to you." . . . So I said, "Milton, what has this little man got to lose?" He walked away. . . . My own parents I couldn't have treated better than I treated all these little sick people.

––––––––

Sarah Cohen Berman served as president of the Minneapolis Talmud Torah Auxiliary in the early 1920s. Her assertions about the importance of women in fostering Jewish education, written for the Rosh Hashanah 1922 issue of the Twin Cities newspaper American Jewish World, *are representative of a large shift in traditional gender roles.*

[T]he largest and most flourishing Jewish woman's organization of Minneapolis has as its chief aim the furtherance of Jewish education. . . . Starting humbly eleven years ago, as a mothers' club . . . it has grown to a membership of more than five hundred. . . . [W]omen realize . . . that the future of Judaism and Jewish education will be largely in their hands, for the men are too much engrossed in the struggle for existence, so that the training of the children devolves more and more upon the mother.

––––––––

Ida Cook, the wife of Rabbi Isaac Cook, is considered the founder of the Duluth Talmud Torah; in 1955 it was renamed the Ida Cook Hebrew School. As her daughter Etta Cook Josephs recalled, Ida worked zealously to maintain the school during her life and provided it with scholarships through her will.

Several mortgages were paid off by Mother (I think) so the building could be called their own. A Talmud Torah Sisterhood was organized in 1903. Mother was elected president. . . . She gave of her time, energy and means. . . . She sacrificed many luxuries . . . even going out to collect funds when she was 96 years old, so that the spirit of Judaism might live.

———

Although Fannie Overman Goldfine of Duluth was heavily involved first in her family's cattle business and later in its furniture store between the early 1920s and the 1960s, she did not neglect her community responsibilities—as her son Manley recalled.

Fannie was famous for her special interests, Talmud Torah being one of them. Each year they sponsored the Purim Ball and for many years, she was either honorary or actual ticket chairman. She handled the "guyum" [non-Jewish] tickets and all the banks, wholesale houses . . . began to expect her once a year when she would take a day or two off work, make the rounds, and sell hundreds of tickets.

LATER AUXILIARIES:
MOUNT SINAI HOSPITAL AUXILIARY

Minneapolis's Mount Sinai Hospital Auxiliary developed a distinctive spirit and innovative fund-raising techniques that made it a model for other local hospital auxiliaries. Muriel Wexler was auxiliary president in the mid-1970s when she wrote a retrospective report that was printed in the Mount Sinai newsletter.

[O]ur Auxiliary was formed by women with vital concerns, foresight and plans for the hospital even before the doors of Mount Sinai were opened.

Our Coffee Shop was their project . . . they were the cooks, waitresses and bottle washers. They opened a Gift Shop, were "play ladies," sold baby photos, worked with patients, promoted their own cookbook, played recordings for patients, serviced the patients with a library cart, gift cart, craft cart, provided escort service, delivered flowers and all the other many duties that only a volunteer can provide. They were concerned and worked to make the hospital more attractive with pictures, plants and furnishings. They initiated the Annual "Birthday" Ball to raise money for hospital care for the indigent.

WOMEN'S DIVISION OF FEDERATION

Theresa Ackerman Berman proved herself as president of the NCJW's Minneapolis section in the late 1950s. In the late 1970s, after serving as the Minneapolis federation women's division president, she became the first female president of the Minneapolis federation board.

There was a great deal of leadership training in the Association [of Jewish Women's Organizations] before it became the Women's

Marsha Tankenoff (right), Ruth Usem (center), and an unidentified woman in a publicity photo for the Mount Sinai Hospital Auxiliary's Mad Hatter's Ball, 1968

Division of the Federation. Now it is very strong. I remember we developed workshops that were very well attended. . . . I was chair of the Central Planning and Budgeting Committee [CPBC]. Then I was the first female President of [the] Federation [in 1978]. . . . I had no difficulty in working with men, either on CPBC or as President.

INDEPENDENT WOMEN'S ORGANIZATIONS:
NATIONAL COUNCIL OF JEWISH WOMEN

Nina Morais Cohen was the daughter of Rabbi Sabato Morais, who helped found the Jewish Theological Seminary in New York City. After her death in 1918 the Minneapolis section of the NCJW, the Woman's Club of Minneapolis, the Minnesota Woman Suffrage Association, the Minneapolis Public Library, and the College Women's Club coauthored an article about her.

[S]he was a unique figure in this new commercial western town. . . . She delivered, in col[l]aboration with a friend, six open lectures on Dante—later a course on Ibsen—all of which are still remembered by many of her listeners as among the germinating forces of the intellectual life of Minneapolis. Her most important work was a series of talks on the Bible, given at the public library. Into this bygone history she instilled the spirit of life. . . .

Since her girlhood, she has been convinced of the justice of women's demands for their full emancipation and development; and even before her marriage she wrote a series of articles on woman suffrage for the North American Review. When Susan B. Anthony and Anna Howard Shaw attended the National Suffrage conference in Minneapolis in 1901, they met at Mrs. Cohen's home.

———

Nina Cohen developed leadership wherever she found it, as Rose Berman Goldstein's reminiscence of her mother, Sarah, indicates. Sarah Cohen Berman had been forced to leave high school to help support her family.

She became the first North Side woman on the Case Conference Committee of the Jewish Charities and brought them the point of view of the recent immigrants. . . .

The dominant German-Jewish group noticed her ability, and she was invited to become a member of the prestigious Study Circle led by Mrs. Emanuel Cohen for the [National] Council of Jewish Women. It was an honor to be invited to join her group. . . . [H]er most ambitious effort . . . was a study of Russian Jewry in the Pale of Settlement. It took months to prepare and two sessions to present. She was sympathetic enough to the old home to be eager to interpret it aright to her alienated German-Jewish sisters.

———

Fanny Fliegelman Brin of Minneapolis served two terms as national president of the NCJW during the 1930s. She worked with Jane Addams, Carrie Chapman Catt, and other nationally prominent women to promote world peace. She wrote the following for the Saturday Post, *a Jewish newspaper, in 1923.*

[W]e whose function in life centers about creation and education, must with endless toil and perseverance take up this task of moulding public opinion against war as a means of settling international disputes. We must not seek to modify war, but to outlaw it; to make it an international crime. . . .

The National Council of Jewish Women is giving active support to the work of the National Council for Prevention of War. In the formation of classes among its members, in the support of legislation which has direct or indirect bearing upon peace, in the education of public opinion every possible help is given. It is natural that Jewish women should give their fullest support. Is it not the Jew who suffers most during war and after?

———

Viola Hoffman Hymes of Minneapolis had been an educator before her marriage. She threw herself into club work and in 1959 became national president of the NCJW. As she recalled in the 1980s:

Fanny Brin (left), Jane Addams,
Hannah Solomon (founder of
the national NCJW), and
Mrs. Gershon Levi at an NCJW
convention in Chicago, 1934

I became pregnant five months after we were married, and Bea
Grossman . . . was pregnant [as well] so we became co-editors of
the Bulletin [newsletter] in the Minneapolis section [of the NCJW].
And made our annual report in June that we produced two babies
and eight bulletins. . . . Fanny Brin . . . was really my mentor. . . .
She persuaded me to be chairman of International Relations, so I
took that on for a couple of years. . . . [O]ur senior citizen activities expanded tremendously [as did] our study groups. . . . And
now, of course, we've moved into this question of battered
women and are much concerned about the needs and welfare of
women.

———

*Marice Lipschultz Halper was president of the St. Paul section of
the NCJW in 1960, and in 1981 she became president of the*

International Council of Jewish Women. Her explanations of how she became active and of the benefits of training and involvement are instructive.

Every bride got a membership, and I was on the legislative and bulletin committees. The legislative committee alerted state and local groups to advocate for the issues Council had taken a stance on—Equal Rights Amendment, equal opportunities for women, fighting [Senator Joseph] McCarthy. We partnered a lot of stuff with League of Women Voters.

Four past presidents of the St. Paul chapter and Viola Hymes, the National President, . . . wanted me to consider becoming the president because the chapter needed revitalization. I said, "absolutely not." . . . Finally, Annette Green, a past president, said, . . . "opportunities like this don't come to . . . anybody except just occasionally in a lifetime." This intrigued me. It was in 1960, and my children were ten and twelve. . . .

The other hook was a leadership training institute. . . . Just for Council women. We did not discuss NCJW, but leadership, motivational behavior, conflict resolution, et cetera. Leadership training in Council changed my life . . . that training and my father dying the year I took the presidency. And I then had a stroke. They did not let me give up presidency.

After that I must have decided that I could do anything. I accepted several governors' appointments to statewide commissions. . . . Viola Hymes . . . was my mentor, [as well as] others in St. Paul [who] had different skills and agreed to oversee those areas while I was president in order to build up leadership. . . . [During the 1960s] we were trying to achieve a standard of equal opportunity for people who didn't have access to power. . . . [W]e were piloting the Headstart [sic] program, the intention being that we were going to help "those people" into the mainstream— "those people" being a specific choice of words on my part. . . . [We] came to understand that type of intervention was not appropriate any longer. . . . What was important was that volunteers were trained at a professional level. . . . [It] empowered and enabled women to return to work.

———

Ruth Rauch Peilen of Minneapolis decided to become involved in the NCJW in the mid-1940s because the organization "emphasized justice . . . and human welfare and civil liberties and all of those concrete things about Judaism" that she found important. Her recollections of alliances among liberal women's groups working for the preservation of basic American rights provide some evidence to refute the idea that the 1950s was a decade in which no significant women's activism occurred. They also show that the NCJW played a role alongside other liberal women's organizations.

[D]uring the McCarthy era there was a great need for a better understanding of individual liberties and how we defend them. And so I devised a program called the Minneapolis Freedom Fair Agenda Program and invited various women's organizations . . . to join us . . . [T]he YWCA decided [to] jointly produce this program [along with] the Minneapolis League of Women Voters, the Council of Church Women, the [Fifth District] Federation of Women's Clubs, Hadassah, the Faculty Women's Club of the University of Minnesota, the Unitarian Woman's Alliance, the Quota Club, the Zonta, the International League for Peace and Freedom, the Association of Jewish Women's Organizations, and the Minnesota State Council of [the] CIO Auxiliary. . . . [A]nd that took a great deal of organization [because] we really wanted to stimulate amongst all of us an appreciation of our freedoms, an understanding of what is at stake, and what happens when we . . . become intolerant of those who have different views. . . . We had monthly study groups, panels, and moderators, and it was a very, very successful program. . . . It cost us a hundred dollars, I think.

HADASSAH

The minutes book of the Sioux Falls, South Dakota, Hadassah chapter for 1923 and 1924 enumerates donations of work and money to Jewish children in Palestine, reflecting a pattern strikingly similar to that of the Protestant women's missionary movement. But the book also reveals something about the chapter's relations with non-Jewish women and about its legislative concerns.

The Sioux Falls chapter of Hadassah provided Seders for servicemen at the nearby airbase during World War II.

June 7, 1923 Lacking machines for sewing, the members worked by hand on infants shirts, three dozen of which were distributed among the members to complete at home. . . .

January 30, 1924 The subject of raising funds to be sent to Palestine for the Hadassah Medical Organization was discussed, and the milk bottle plan was adopted. The secretary to send for six such bottles, to be distributed among the Jewish societies here, requesting pennies to be dropped into the little bottle at each of their meetings. . . . Said bottles to be collected once every three months. . . . Resolutions were signed by all members protesting against the Johnson bill of Immigration, and duly forwarded to Sen. Thos. Sterling, Sen. Peter Norbeck, and our Rep. of Dist. No. 2.*

———

*The Johnson-Reed Act of 1924, which severely restricted Eastern and Southern European immigration, ended the great European Jewish migration to the United States.

*Hadassah did more than raise funds. In a small town such as
Sioux Falls, service to Jewish soldiers was within its purview as well,
as the chapter scrapbook from the 1940s makes clear.*

It being impossible to accommodate [the soldiers] for the
Passover seders at home, we proceeded with the help of the Army
to conduct the seders at the base. At each Seder we took care of
800 boys. The overflow were taken to Sioux City[, and] it took
practically all the local women and many of the wives visiting the
base to carry the project out.

––––––––

*Anne Garon Greenberg was president of the St. Paul chapter of
Hadassah in 1945. In 1954 she began to work full time at the
Ramsey County Welfare Department.*

[W]e'd raise money [by giving] a dinner. And the women used
to do their own cooking in those days. . . . Rose Rosenthal, a
woman who could do everything, rolled up her sleeves and was
making stuffed baked potatoes. And I was washing dishes . . .
and I looked at my hands and they were wrinkled like a prune.
. . . But later on we became a little fancier and we had caterers to
help us. . . .

But every summer was ruined for me because I had to get committees. . . . You sit on the phone and talk to people, and you
know how [to] get a chairman of a committee don't you? . . .
[W]ell I used to talk to them and flatter them. . . . I never would
have had the education I got [except] by working in Hadassah
and on the boards of the [Jewish Community] Center and the
activities that I had in community work. . . . I learned how to
write a letter [, and] I learned a lot about finances and planning,
about programming.

––––––––

*Marilyn Mankoff Rovner, like Marice Halper, emphasized the fel-
lowship as well as the status of belonging to a woman's organiza-*

In the mid-1960s, Rose Rosenthal (left), Ethel Levey, an unidentified woman, Sophie Dudovitz, Sylvia Lipshultz, and Edith Rutman were among the St. Paul Hadassah chapter members who relied heavily on the telephone to build membership, recruit volunteers, and arrange large-scale luncheons.

tion. She became active in the Minneapolis chapter of Hadassah during the post-World War II era.

You were part of the "in group" to be on the board. . . . Roz [Rosalyn Baker] was the chapter president and she invited me onto the board to be the chapter rummage chairman, and I was so flattered and so excited I didn't know what to do. . . . The minyan was a vehicle for raising funds for Youth Aliyah—but it was a support group.* . . . We discussed children, marriages, and deaths.

JEWISH WOMEN'S ORGANIZATIONS IN SMALL TOWNS

Women who lived in small towns had special problems—for instance, trying to maintain a variety of organizations with a

---

*Hadassah minyans are small activity groups that meet regularly and donate funds to the Youth Aliyah, which supports children's educational needs in Israel.

limited number of people. Rhana Lewis was born in Chisholm, Minnesota, in the 1910s. After her marriage to Morris Greenberg in 1935, she lived most of her life in nearby Eveleth on the Mesabi Iron Range.

At first we had a CJW [Council of Jewish Women] and a Hadassah, but it was just the same girls doing the same thing only doing it twice. So we, in spite of opposition from nationals, we merged to the Virginia-Eveleth Council/Hadassah. . . . We told them if they want us to belong they have to take us on our terms because we just cannot maintain two separate organizations. Then we merged with the Ladies' Aid.

————

Jewish women in small towns were active in nonsectarian organizations as well. Often their degree of involvement was related to the amount of anti-Semitism they perceived. Rhana Greenberg's qualifications as a former schoolteacher and status as the wife of a prominent local lawyer positioned her for inclusion in the local Woman's Club.

On the Range the Jewish people belonged to women's clubs, men's clubs, Eastern Star, musical groups, whatever they were interested in. . . . The Woman's Club here at first did not accept Jewish women. In fact, I was the first Jewish woman to join . . . I was asked . . . and I accepted the challenge and there was no problem.

————

Marion Newman's recollections of his mother Sarah's activities in the small Minnesota town of Brainerd were indicative of community leaders' flexible attitudes: Once a Jewish person had proven her civic worth, she tended to be accepted.

My mother was a very liberated woman. She took care of her household duties and she worked part-time . . . in my dad's store.

She . . . became president of the PTA [and] became president of the Woman's Club in Brainerd. She was very highly regarded. [I]n 1933, when some forty percent of the working people in Brainerd . . . were unemployed . . . they couldn't get any businessman in town to accept the chairmanship of the community drive. They came to my mother. This was revolutionary. Nobody ever heard of a woman taking on such a job, but she did.

JEWISH WOMEN AND CIVIC WORK IN THE CITIES

Viola Hoffman Hymes, a former schoolteacher, became active in lobbying for improvement of public education in 1934, was president of the Citizen's Committee on Public Education from 1953 to 1955 and was elected to the Minneapolis school board in 1963.

Well, the first Citizen's Committee on Public Education was formed in Minneapolis. . . . And that was made up primarily of [b]oth men['s] and women's organizations. . . . I became very active in this charter group . . . which was for the support of Minneapolis public schools, which were in dire straits financially.

WORKING FOR MULTIPLE ORGANIZATIONS

Millie King Goldstone grew up on Minneapolis's North Side during the 1930s. Her memories of how she became involved in organizations are typical.

My first organization was Hadassah. My friends and sister were involved. I worked at fundraising. From there I got active in Federation. I was active when they used to go down to the Gymal Doled [Club] and take cards [for solicitation] on Sunday morning and go door to door. I always believed in volunteerism. . . . My mother was the first president of the Emanuel Cohen Center Auxiliary [the first Minneapolis Jewish Community Center] and active in other organizations such as Community Chest, so it has always been in my house.

I was Israel Bond chairman the same time as I was President-elect of the Mount Sinai Auxiliary and Chair of the Federation

Women's Division. My husband finally put a phone in the bathroom, because whenever I went in the phone would ring.

My secret is that I am well organized and I had time.

CHANGING TIMES

Irma Cain graduated from Vassar in 1907, taught school, and volunteered at Chicago's Hull House before marrying Milton Firestone. She served two terms as president of the NCJW's St. Paul section during the 1930s. She was active in at least a score of other organizations as well. Her daughter, Ruth Firestone Brin, recalled some of her mother's tasks.

My mother was also Chairman of the Central Community House . . . and she was Chairman of Sophie Wirth Camp for Council [NCJW] for many years. . . . [She] was imbued with the idea that the members of the Jewish community that had means and education owed a great deal to those who didn't. . . . The major change, that I see, is that women like my mother and Fanny Brin, who were college graduates in a period when most Jewish women did not have that opportunity, worked practically full time at volunteer jobs, and those jobs were high quality jobs. They were doing professional jobs for no pay. Today, [those] jobs are done by professionals, and what the volunteer is asked to do [is] either be on a board where a few policy decisions are made or else do [low-grade] volunteer work.

———

Millie Goldstone found a solution to the dilemma of the educated woman: She combined a professional career with one of voluntarism.

I started counseling at Meadowbrook [Women's Health Center] nineteen years ago doing pre-abortion counseling. . . . Before I became the President of Women's Division of the Federation in 1974 I wanted to see if I was still marketable. The first year they didn't hire me. Right after I took the Presidency they hired [me].

They worked around my schedule which had loads of meetings around the [federation] campaign. The hospital [commitment as president-elect of Mount Sinai Hospital Auxiliary] was full time as well. Now I have gone back to work two days a week.

———

Marice Halper gives a cogent answer to women who feel that organizational work is not rewarding. In the mid-1990s, after more than forty years of volunteer service, she continues to be involved in national and international NCJW projects. In addition to other such activities, she has served on the boards of the St. Paul Foundation and the American National Bank in St. Paul.

Why would I at this age . . . and with many other opportunities offered me . . . consider pursuing this avenue of organizational involvement? [It is because I still enjoy the] fulfilling part of the activity itself, [and] being connected to like-minded women, being inspired and drawing strength from them.

Bibliography

Note to the reader: Sources for "Voices" used in this book are indicated by an asterisk.

COLLECTIONS

AJA . . . . American Jewish Archives, Cincinnati, Ohio

HUC-JIR . . . . Hebrew Union College–Jewish Institute of Religion, Cincinnati, Ohio

JHSUM . . . . Jewish Historical Society of the Upper Midwest, St. Paul
Collections, including:
    PDJSMC . . . . Project to Document Jewish Settlers in Minnesota Collection
    NCJWMSC . . . . National Council of Jewish Women, Minneapolis Section, Collection
    NDJHPC . . . . North Dakota Jewish Historical Project Collection
    UJFCC . . . . United Jewish Fund and Council Collection

MHS . . . . Minnesota Historical Society, St. Paul
Collections, including:
    Ida Blehert Davis Papers

PC . . . . Private collection of Linda Mack Schloff

SHSND . . . . State Historical Society of North Dakota, Bismarck
Collections, including:
    Alfred A. Thal Collection

USD . . . . University of South Dakota, Vermillion
Collections, including:
    SDOHP . . . . South Dakota Oral History Project, South Dakota Oral History Center

MANUSCRIPTS

*Baker, Rachel Minenberg. "A Homesteader in North Dakota." N.d. NDJHPC, JHSUM.

*Bellin, Craney Goldman. "Journey to Freedom." N.d. NDJHPC, JHSUM.

*Bernstein, Ethel Krochock. "Our Family History." Ca. 1975. NDJHPC, JHSUM.

Covner, Thelma C. "The New Wilderness: Building the Jewish Community in Duluth, Minnesota, 1870–1975." 1975. JHSUM; MHS.

*Davis, Ida Blehert. "Memoirs of a Jewish Social [W]orker in St. Paul." N.d. Davis Papers, MHS.

*Deutsch, Marlchen. As told by Amos Deinard in "Mrs. Marlchen Deutsch: An Interview." Ca. late 1920s. JHSUM.

*Dolf, Samuel. "Abraham Dolf." Ca. 1975. NDJHPC, JHSUM.

*Edelman, Edith Modelevsky Linoff. "History of My Life." Nov. 21, 1923. PC of Edelman.

*Freedland, Morris. "From Potatoes to Penicillin." 1989. JHSUM.

*Geller, Toba Marcowitz. "Our Family." Ca. 1976. NDJHPC, JHSUM.

*Gidding, Florence Silberstein. "Origin of Duluth's First Reformed Jewish Sunday School." N.d. JHSUM.

*Giller, Norton. "The Giller Family: History of the Immigration of the Giller Family to North Dakota." Ca. Nov. 22, 1975. NDJHPC, JHSUM.

*Goldfine, Manley. Letter to Linda Mack Schloff, Aug. 25, 1992. JHSUM.

*_____, comp. "Recollections by the Family of Rose and Sander Goldfine." 1991. JHSUM.

*Goldman, Rose Barzon. As told by Daniel J. Elazar in "Aunt Rose: A Memoir." Mar. 5, 1975. MHS.

*Goodman, Pearl Borow. "Family History of Max and Bella Borow." Ca. 1976. NDJHPC, JHSUM.

*Greenstein, Hyman. "The Start of the Greenstein Dynasty." 1954–55. JHSUM.

*Gusack, Rita Pomerance. "The Machowsky and Pomerance Families." Ca. 1975–76. NDJHPC, JHSUM.

Hadassah, Minneapolis Chapter. Historical clippings file, 1930s–90s. Minutes, 1948–49, 1956–73, 1981–85. JHSUM.

Hadassah, St. Paul Chapter. Minutes. 1949–74. JHSUM.

*Hadassah, Sioux Falls, S.Dak., Chapter. Minutes and scrapbook. 1923–24. PC of Chapter.

*Handelman, Leo. "The Handelman Story." N.d. NDJHPC, JHSUM.

*Hebrew Ladies Aid Society, Fargo, N.Dak. Minutes. 1904–17, transcription, JHSUM. 1919–32, microfilm, AJA.

Hebrew Ladies Benevolent Society, St. Paul. Minutes. 1881–83, 1891–99. MHS.

Herbst, Robert B.? "Herbst Family." Ca. 1978. NDJHPC, JHSUM.

*Josephs, Etta Cook. Untitled manuscript for speech. Ca. 1955. JHSUM.

*Ladies Aid Society, Virginia, Minn. Minutes. 1908–13. JHSUM.

*Levin, Rose. "The Philip and Sarah Levin Family." Sept. 1976. NDJHPC, JHSUM.

*Losk, Charles. Journal. 1947. AJA.

*Mains, Daisy Ginsburg. "The Grandparent's Book: Answers to a Grandchild's Questions." Dec. 8, 1977. JHSUM.

*Mann, Rochele Gela. As told by Albert Mann in "The Rubel-Mann Families." Ca. 1977. AJA; NDJHPC, JHSUM.

*Mesonznick, Edith Guttman. Letter to Beatrice Premack, Oct. 30, 1987 (photocopy). JHSUM.

Minneapolis Federation for Jewish Service, Women's Division. Minutes and reports. 1947–50, 1953–60, 1965. JHSUM.

Mount Sinai Hospital Auxiliary, Minneapolis. Minutes. 1950–91. JHSUM.

National Council of Jewish Women, Minneapolis Section. Annual reports and membership directories, 1935–95. Minutes, 1950–81. JHSUM.

National Council of Jewish Women, St. Paul Section. Minutes, 1930–69. President's papers, 1969–82. JHSUM.

*Overby, Ethel Schlasinger. "Noah and Sarah Schlasinger." Ca. 1977. NDJHPC, JHSUM.

Premack, Beatrice. "A History of the Jewish Community of Aberdeen, South Dakota, 1887–1964." N.d. JHSUM.

*Rodd, Emily Zvorist. "Morris and Ghisela Zvorist." Feb. 20, 1976. NDJHPC, JHSUM.

*Rosen, Anna Labovich. "Events on the Farm in North Dakota as I Remember Them." N.d. JHSUM.

*Rosenberg, Betty. "William and Betty Rosenberg." Ca. 1976. NDJHPC, JHSUM.

*Rosenberg, Sylvia Kremen. "The Story of a Homesteader and His Family." 1976. NDJHPC, JHSUM.

*Rosenthal, Rose. As told by Selma Goldish in "History of Duluth Senior Hadassah." N.d. JHSUM.

*Saval, Jeanette Kopelman. Letter to Toba Geller, June 27, 1977. NDJHPC, JHSUM.

*Schlasinger, Noah. As told by Ethel Schlasinger Overby in "Noah and Sarah Schlasinger." Ca. 1977. NDJHPC, JHSUM.

Schloff, Linda Mack. "Kosher with a Modern Tinge: Two Generations of Jewish Women in Virginia, Minnesota, 1894–1945." 1984. PC.

*Schwartz, Bessie Halpern. "My Own Story." 1956. AJA; NDJHPC, JHSUM.

*Schwartz, Rose Rapaport. "Sam and Pearl Rapaport." Ca. 1976. NDJHPC, JHSUM.

*Shalett, Sarah Yager. As told by Sherna Shalett Vinograd in "A Story of That Time." N.d. AJA.

*Sher, Florence Shuman. "Reminiscences." 1976. MHS.

*Sherman, Elizabeth Banick. "The Banick and Fishman Families." 1977. NDJHPC, JHSUM.

*Silberstein, Janet. "Daughters of Abraham Sisterhood." 1987. JHSUM.

*Strosberg, James M. Letter to Beatrice Premack, Oct. 26, 1987 (photocopy). PC.

*Supak, Sophie Katz. As told by Paul Kleyman in "Shifra: Her Early Years." 1986. JHSUM.

*Sweed, Rose Mill. "Israel's Castle." 1977. NDJHPC, JHSUM.

*Tenenbaum, Morris. "The Family History." N.d. JHSUM.

*Thal, Sarah. As written by Martha Thal in "Early Days: The Story of Sarah Thal: Wife of a Pioneer Farmer of Nelson County, N.D." N.d. JHSUM.

*Ullmann, Amelia (Mrs. Joseph). "Saint Paul Forty Years Ago." 1896. AJA; MHS. Portions published in *Minnesota History* as "Spring Comes to the Frontier," vol. 33 (Spring 1953): 194–200, "Frontier Business Trip," 34 (Spring 1954): 17–27, and "Pioneer Homemaker," 34 (Autumn 1954): 96–105. Excerpts published as "Frontier Days on the Upper Mississippi," in *Memoirs of American Jews, 1775–1865,* comp. and ed. Jacob Rader Marcus (3 vols.; The Jacob R. Schiff Library of Jewish Contributions to American Democracy; Philadelphia: Jewish Publication Society of America) 2 (1955): 351–75.

United States. Manuscript census schedules, 1910, for North Side, Minneapolis, and West Side and Capitol areas, St. Paul. Microfilm, MHS.

*Vinograd, Sherna Shalett. "A Story of That Time." N.d. AJA.

Weber, Laura. "Minneapolis Jews and Employment: 1930–1950; With Emphasis on the Depression Era." Paper in fulfillment of M.A. requirement, University of Minnesota, 1982. JHSUM.

*Werner, Nellie Brody. "The Brody Family." Ca. 1976. NDJHPC, JHSUM.

*Women's League, Temple of Aaron, St. Paul. Minutes. 1941–55. JHSUM.

ORAL HISTORIES

The interviewer's name follows the date. Unless otherwise noted, the interviewer is Linda Mack Schloff.

*Abrahamson, Elka. Feb. 7, 1995. PC.

*Agrant, Jeannette L. Sept. 11, 1976; Freda Hosen. SDOHP 1108, USD.

*Aronson, David. As told by Guita Gordon, Aug. 17, 1993. PC.

*Bailin, Solomon. Aug. 28, 1974; Freda Hosen. SDOHP 1189, USD.

*Baker, Rosalyn, Fredell Cohen, and Marilyn Mankoff Rovner. Aug. 19, 1993. PC.

*Balick, Ida. Aug. 9, 1977; Gladys Zisson. UJFCC, JHSUM.

*Banen, Bernice, and Sadie Gallagher. Oct. 20, 1981; Marilyn J. Chiat. PDJSMC, JHSUM.

*Berlin, Carol Porter. July 22, 1994. PC.

*Berman, Theresa Ackerman. Aug. 12, 1993. PC.

*Borsten, Laura Rapaport, and Rose Rapaport Schwartz. June 9, 1994. PC.

*Brezman, Inna Gendelman. July 18, 1991. PC.

*Brin, Ruth Firestone. Oct. 8, 1986; Ruth Peilen. NCJWMSC, JHSUM.

*Dokovna, Joe. Dec. 20, 1972; Alfred A. Thal. Thal Collection, SHSND.

*Dreytser, Galina Khaikina. Nov. 14, 1991. PC.

*Field, Gladys Jacobs. Jan. 29, 1978; Rhoda G. Lewin. MHS.

Frishberg, Sarah. Oct. 26, 1977; Miriam Frishberg. UJFCC, JHSUM.

*Gillman, Rose, Gertrude Devitt, and Sid Selsberg. May 21, 1978; Lois Devitt. UJFCC, JHSUM.

*Golberg, Ida Cohen. Nov. 6, 1981; Siegbert Woll-stein. PDJSMC, JHSUM.

*Goldberg, Blanche Halpern. 1976; Rhoda G. Lewin. MHS.

*Goldstone, Millie King. Nov. 16, 1993. PC.

*Gordon, Julie. Feb. 28, 1995. PC.

*Greenberg, Anne Garon. Mar. 28, 1978; Lois Devitt. UJFCC, JHSUM.

*Greenberg, Rhana Lewis. July 19, 1983; Cindy Held. PDJSMC, JHSUM.

*Halper, Marice Lipschultz. June 28, 1994. PC.

*Hurwitz, Dorothy Mosow. May 3, 1994. PC.

*Hymes, Viola Hoffman. Dec. 8, 1986; Idell Silberman. NCJWMSC, JHSUM.

*Kamins, Celia. N.d.; unknown interviewer. NDJHPC, JHSUM.

*Levy, Eva. July 9, 1978; Anne Greenberg. UJFCC, JHSUM.

*Marcowitz, Frieda Aurach, and Julia Lewis. Oct. 13, 1973; Alfred A. Thal. Thal Collection, SHSND.

*Marsh, Cecyle Eirinberg. May 3, 1994. PC.

Milavetz, Edith. Mar. 1978; Judy Aronson. UJFCC, JHSUM.

*Milavetz, Frances Kaufman. July 20, 1983; Roxane Markoff. PDJSMC, JHSUM.

*Newman, Marion. June 18, 1987; Marilyn J. Chiat. PDJSMC, JHSUM.

*Overbach, Rose Levy. June 6, 1988; Marilyn J. Chiat. PDJSMC, JHSUM.

*Peilen, Ruth Rauch. Jan. 8, 1987; Percy Bloom. NCJWMSC, JHSUM.

*Peilen, Sylvia Feinstein. Apr. 13, 1978; Anne Greenberg. UJFCC, JHSUM.

*Pertzik, Marvin, and other community leaders. June 12, 1984; Lois Devitt, moderator. UJFCC, JHSUM.

*Pitts, Isadore. Aug. 24, 1974; Freda Hosen. SDOHP 1187, USD.

*Rauch, Belle Woolpy. July 26, 1986; Joan E. Schore. NCJWMSC, JHSUM.

*Rosenauer, Sophia Shankman. July 11, 1991. PC.

*Rovner, Marilyn Mankoff, Rosalyn Baker, and Fredell Cohen. Aug. 19, 1993. PC.

*Sanders, Ida Levitan. 1976; Rhoda G. Lewin. MHS.

*Schanfield, Fannie Schwartz. Interviewed in Minnesota Public Radio documentary "No Jews Allowed"; John Biewen and Beth Friend, producers. Broadcast Sept. 21, 1992. Copy of sound recording, JHSUM.

*Shark, Myer. Oct. 23, 1979; conversation with Howard Nelson. NDJHPC, JHSUM.

*Shuirman, Theodore. Oct. 15, 1981. PDJSMC, JHSUM.

*Sinitsky, Jane. June 9, 1991; Schloff and Dianne Siegel. PC.

*Smirnov, Nadia Ackerman. Dec. 10, 1991. PC.

*Stacker, Ralph. N.d.; Andy Gellman. UJFCC, JHSUM.

*Straus, Rose Feldman, and Al Straus. Nov. 26, 1977; Tom Newgard. NDJHPC, JHSUM.

*Supak, Sophie Katz. Oct. 1974; Paul Kleyman. JHSUM.

*Waldman, Cecilia Rose. Feb. 28, 1995. PC.

*Zabel, Anne Rothenberg. May 2, 1994. PC.

NEWSPAPERS AND PERIODICALS

American Hebrew (New York). HUC-JIR.

American Jewish World (Minneapolis). JHSUM; MHS.

Hadassah, Minneapolis Chapter. *Hadassah Bulletin* (variant title: *Hadassah Monthly*). 1941–69. JHSUM. *Hadassah Lifeline.* 1969–93. JHSUM.

Hadassah, St. Paul Chapter. *Bulletin.* 1960–69. JHSUM; MHS. *This Is Hadassah.* 1969–82. JHSUM; MHS.

Mount Sinai Hospital, Minneapolis. *Mount Sinai Hospital Messenger* (variant titles: *Messenger, Messenger: Mount Sinai Hospital Newsletter*). 1955–84. JHSUM; MHS. *Mount Sinai Hospital News.* 1949. JHSUM.

National Council of Jewish Women, Minneapolis Section. *Bulletin* (variant titles: *Council Bulletin, Minneapolis Bulletin, Minneapolis*

Section, *Minneapolis Section Bulletin, NCJW Bulletin*). 1924–94. JHSUM; MHS.

National Council of Jewish Women, St. Paul Section. *Bulletin* (variant titles: *Council Bulletin, NCJW Bulletin, Saint Paul Section Bulletin*). 1938–87. JHSUM; MHS.

Reform Advocate (Chicago). HUC-JIR.

Saturday Post: The Northwestern Jewish Weekly (Minneapolis and St. Paul). JHSUM; MHS.

BOOKS, BOOKLETS, AND THESES

*Apple, Slovie Solomon. *They Were Strangers: A Family History.* New York: Vantage Press, 1995. JHSUM; MHS.

*Bachrach, Jeanette Wrottenberg. *Above Rubies.* Los Angeles: Globe Printing Co., 1933. AJA.

Baron, Salo W. *The Russian Jew under Tsars and Soviets.* New York: Macmillan, 1964.

Baum, Charlotte, Paula [E.] Hyman, and Sonya Michel. *The Jewish Woman in America.* New York: Dial Press, 1976. Reprint. New York: New American Library, Plume Books, 1977.

*Berger, Benjamin N. As told by Robert K. Krishef in *Thank You, America: The Biography of Benjamin N. Berger.* Minneapolis: Dillon Press, 1982. JHSUM; MHS.

Berman, Hyman. "The Jews." In *They Chose Minnesota,* ed. Holmquist. P. 489–507.

*Berman, Sarah Cohen. "Call Me Marah." [Minneapolis]: Privately printed, 1991. JHSUM.

*Bernstein, Leah Lisovsky. *Leah: For Freedom—For Love—: Autobiography of Leah Lisovsky Bernstein.* Robbinsdale, Minn.: Privately printed, 1986. JHSUM; MHS.

Borchert, John R. *America's Northern Heartland.* Minneapolis: University of Minnesota Press, 1987.

Budish, J. M., and George Soule. *The New Unionism in the Clothing Industry.* New York: Harcourt, Brace and Howe, 1920. MHS.

*Calof, Rachel Bella Kahn. *Rachel Calof's Story: Jewish Homesteader on the Northern Plains.* Trans. Jacob Calof and Molly Shaw; ed. J. Sanford Rikoon. Bloomington: Indiana University Press, 1995.

*Char, Sam. "Memories of a Young Jewish Immigrant." In "To Commemorate Jewish Book Month," comp. Members of the Leisure League of the St. Paul Jewish Community Center, n.d. P. 1–6. JHSUM.

Chiat, Marilyn J., and Chester Proshan. *We Rolled up Our Sleeves: A History of the United Jewish Fund and Council of Saint Paul and Its Beneficiary Agencies.* St. Paul: The Fund and Council, 1985. JHSUM; MHS.

Dobkowski, Michael N. *Jewish American Voluntary Organizations.* Westport, Conn.: Greenwood Press, 1986.

*Edelman, Edith Modelevsky Linoff. *The Wisdom of Love: An Autobiography.* Minneapolis: EMLE, 1981. JHSUM; MHS.

Encyclopaedia Judaica. 16 vols. Jerusalem: Encyclopaedia Judaica; [New York]: Macmillan, [1971–72].

Gitelman, Zvi. *A Century of Ambivalence: The Jews of Russia and the Soviet Union, 1881 to the Present.* New York: Schocken Books, 1988.

Glenn, Susan A. *Daughters of the Shtetl: Life and Labor in the Immigrant Generation.* Ithaca: Cornell University Press, 1990.

Goering, Orlando J., and Violet Goering. "Jews of South Dakota: The Adaptation of a Unique Ethnic Minority." In *14th Dakota History Conference: April 2 and 3, 1982: Papers,* comp. H. W. Blakely. Karl E. Mundt Historical & Educational Foundation Series, no. 10. Madison, S.Dak.: Dakota State College, 1983. P. 215–43.

*Goldstein, Rose Berman. "Memories of Sarah." In "Sarah and Alexander Berman: A Family Chronicle, by Their Children," by Sarah Cohen Berman. [Minneapolis?: Privately printed, 1973]. P. 35–102. JHSUM; MHS.

Gordon, Albert I. *Jews in Transition.* Minneapolis: University of Minnesota Press, 1949.

Goren, Arthur A. "Jews." In *Harvard Encyclopedia of American Ethnic Groups,* ed. Stephan Thernstrom. Cambridge, Mass.: Belknap Press, 1980. P. 571–98.

Hadassah, Hibbing-Chisholm, Minn., Chapter. *Hot off the Range.* Lenexa, Kans.: Cookbook Publishers, 1981. PC.

*Hallock, Kopple. "Steps along the Way: A Walk through Eightysomething Years of My Life." Privately printed, 1989. JHSUM.

Heinze, Andrew R. *Adapting to Abundance: Jewish Immigrants, Mass Consumption, and the Search for American Identity.* Columbia History of Urban Life. New York: Columbia University Press, 1990.

Holmquist, June Drenning, ed. *They Chose Minnesota: A Survey of the State's Ethnic Groups.* St. Paul: Minnesota Historical Society Press, 1981.

Howe, Irving. *World of Our Fathers.* New York: Harcourt Brace Jovanovich, 1976.

Hyman, Paula E. "Gender and the Immigrant Jewish Experience in the United States." In *Jewish Women in Historical Perspective,* ed. Judith R. Baskin. Detroit: Wayne State University Press, 1991. P. 222–42.

Joselit, Jenna Weissman. "The Special Sphere of the Middle-Class American Jewish Woman: The Synagogue Sisterhood, 1890–1940." In *The American Synagogue: A Sanctuary Transformed,* ed. Jack Wertheimer. Cambridge and New York: Cambridge University Press, 1987. P. 206–30.

_____. *The Wonders of America: Reinventing Jewish Culture 1880–1950.* New York: Hill and Wang, 1994.

Katz, Jacob. *Out of the Ghetto: The Social Background of Jewish Emancipation, 1770–1870.* Cambridge, Mass.: Harvard University Press,

1973. Reprint. New York: Schocken Books, 1978.

Kirshenblatt-Gimblett, Barbara. "Kitchen Judaism." In *Getting Comfortable in New York: The American Jewish Home, 1880–1950,* ed. Susan L. Braunstein and Jenna Weissman Joselit. New York: The Jewish Museum, 1990. P. 75–105.

Kugelmass, Jack, and Jonathan Boyarin, trans. and eds. *From a Ruined Garden: The Memorial Books of Polish Jewry.* New York: Schocken Books, 1983.

Lazarus, Mitchel J., and Judith B. Erickson. *The Jewish Community of Greater Minneapolis, 1971–1972: A Population Study.* Minneapolis: Central Planning and Budget Committee, Minneapolis Federation for Jewish Service, [1973]. JHSUM; MHS.

Lintelman, Joy K. "More Freedom, Better Pay: Single Swedish Immigrant Women in the United States, 1880–1920." Ph.D. thesis, University of Minnesota, 1991. MHS.

Marinbach, Bernard. *Galveston, Ellis Island of the West.* Albany: State University of New York Press, 1983.

Mendelsohn, Ezra. *Class Struggle in the Pale: The Formative Years of the Jewish Workers' Movement in Tsarist Russia.* Cambridge, England: Cambridge University Press, 1970.

Milton, John. *South Dakota: A Bicentennial History.* The States and the Nation series. New York: W. W. Norton & Co.; Nashville, Tenn.: American Association for State and Local History, 1977.

Minda, Albert G. *The Story of Temple Israel, Minneapolis, Minnesota: A Personal Account.* Minneapolis, 1971. JHSUM; MHS.

Minneapolis Federation for Jewish Service. *Community Self-Survey of Social, Cultural and Recreational Needs: Workbook: A Summary of the Factual Data from the Population Study and Other Sources Necessary for Social Planning Committees.* Minneapolis: The Federation, June 1958. JHSUM.

Plains Folk: North Dakota's Ethnic Heritage. Ed. William C. Sherman and Playford V. Thorson. Fargo: North Dakota Institute for Regional Studies, 1986. MHS.

Plaut, W. Gunther. *The Jews in Minnesota: The First Seventy-five Years.* American Jewish Communal Histories, no. 3. New York: American Jewish Historical Society, 1959. JHSUM; MHS.

_____. *Mount Zion, 1856–1957: The First Hundred Years.* St. Paul: North Central Publishing Co., 1956. JHSUM; MHS.

Rapp, Michael Gerald. "An Historical Overview of Anti-Semitism in Minnesota, 1920–1960: With Particular Emphasis on Minneapolis and St. Paul." Ph.D. thesis, University of Minnesota, 1977. JHSUM; MHS.

Rikoon, J. Sanford. "Jewish Farm Settlements in America's Heartland." In *Rachel Calof's Story*, by Calof. P. 105–33.

Rogow, Faith. *Gone to Another Meeting: The National Council of Jewish Women, 1893–1993.* Judaic Studies Series. Tuscaloosa: University of Alabama Press, 1993.

Roskies, Diane K., and David G. Roskies, comps. *The Shtetl Book: An Introduction to East European Jewish Life and Lore.* New York: Ktav Publishing House, 1975. 2d ed., 1979.

*Roth, Winnie Lewis. Eulogizing Etta Silk Hallock, as quoted by K. Hallock in "Steps along the Way." P. 30–36.

Rubinow, Isaac M. "Economic and Industrial Condition: New York." In *The Russian Jew in the United States: Studies of Social Conditions in New York, Philadelphia, and Chicago, with a Description of Rural Settlements,* ed. Charles S. Bernheimer. Philadelphia: John C. Winston Co., 1905. Reprint. The American Immigration Library. New York: Jerome S. Ozer, 1971. P. 101–21.

_____. *Economic Condition of the Jews in Russia.* Washington, D.C.: GPO, 1907. Reprint. New York: Arno Press, 1975.

Rutman, Herbert Samuel. "Defense and Development: A History of Minneapolis Jewry, 1930–1950." Ph.D. thesis, University of Minnesota, 1970. MHS.

*Ryder, Sara Bashefkin. *Of Thee I Write: I Am a Product of the St. Paul West Side Flats.* New Ulm: Privately printed, 1989. JHSUM; MHS.

Schell, Herbert S. *History of South Dakota.* 3d ed. Lincoln: University of Nebraska Press, 1975.

Schloff, Linda Mack. *Our Story: A History of Hadassah, St. Paul Chapter, 1913–1988.* [Minn., 1988]. JHSUM; MHS.

*Schwarz, Willy. As quoted in *Voices from the Old Country,* comp. Bart Schneider. Minneapolis: Out of Hand Press, Minneapolis College of Art and Design, 1985. Portfolio of unbound, unnumbered sheaves. JHSUM.

Seidman, Joel. *The Needle Trades.* New York: Farrar & Rinehart, 1942.

Sherman, William C. "Jews." In *Plains Folk.* P. 388–406.

_____. *Prairie Mosaic: An Ethnic Atlas of Rural North Dakota.* Fargo: North Dakota Institute for Regional Studies, 1983. MHS.

Singer-Miller, Lael. *Rachel.* [Duluth?, Minn.], 1980. AJA; MHS.

Sklare, Marshall. *Conservative Judaism: An American Religious Movement.* Glencoe, Ill.: Free Press, 1955. New augmented ed. New York: Schocken Books, 1972.

_____, and Joseph Greenblum. *Jewish Identity on the Suburban Frontier: A Study of Group Survival in the Open Society.* New York: Basic Books, 1967.

Slack, Hiram Worchester. *Directory of Charitable and Benevolent Organizations: A Classified and Descriptive Reference Book of the Charitable, Civic, Educational, and Religious*

Resources of Saint Paul, Minnesota: Together with Legal Suggestions. St. Paul: Amherst H. Wilder Charity, 1913. MHS.

Sochen, June. *Consecrate Every Day: The Public Lives of Jewish American Women, 1880–1980.* SUNY Series in Modern Jewish History. Albany: State University of New York Press, 1981.

*Thompson, Era Bell. *American Daughter.* Chicago: University of Chicago Press, 1946. Reprints. Chicago: Follett Publishing Co., 1967. St. Paul: Minnesota Historical Society Press, Borealis Books, 1986.

*Trupin, Sophie Turnoy. *Dakota Diaspora: Memoirs of a Jewish Homesteader.* Berkeley, Calif.: Alternative Press, 1984. Reprint. Lincoln: University of Nebraska Press, Bison Books, 1988.

United States. Immigration Commission (1907–10). *Reports of the Immigration Commission.* 41 vols. Washington, D.C.: GPO, 1911.

Wilkins, Robert P., and Wynona Huchette Wilkins. *North Dakota: A Bicentennial History.* The States and the Nation series. New York: W. W. Norton & Co.; Nashville, Tenn.: American Association for State and Local History, 1977.

ARTICLES

Aronson, I. Michael. "The Attitudes of Russian Officials in the 1880s toward Jewish Assimilation and Emigration." *Slavic Review* 34 (Mar. 1975): 1–18.

———. "The Prospects for the Emancipation of Russian Jewry during the 1880s." *Slavonic and East European Review* 55 (July 1977): 348–69.

*Berman, Sarah Cohen (Mrs. Alexander). "The Ladies' Auxiliary of the Talmud Torah." *American Jewish World* (Minneapolis), Sept. 22, 1922, p. 21. JHSUM; MHS.

*Brin, Fanny Fliegelman (Mrs. Arthur). "Women and the Peace Movement." *Saturday Post: The Northwestern Jewish Weekly* (Minneapolis and St. Paul), Sept. 7, 1923, p. 19. JHSUM; MHS.

*Cohen, Nina Morais. As eulogized by Mollie Jacobs (Mrs. Leopold) Metzger et al. in "An Appreciation: Nina Morais Cohen." *Minneapolis Journal,* Feb. 23, 1918, p. 4.

Cooper, Charles I. "The Jews of Minneapolis and Their Christian Neighbors." *Jewish Social Studies* 8 (Jan. 1946): 31–38.

*Fine, Henry, and Lea Fine. "North Dakota Memories." *Western States Jewish Historical Quarterly* 9 (July 1977): 331–40.

Goering, Orlando J., and Violet Goering. "Jewish Farmers in South Dakota—The Am Olam." *South Dakota History* 12 (Winter 1982): 232–47.

"History of the Jews of Duluth." *Reform Advocate* (Chicago), special issue (photocopy). JHSUM.

"History of the Jews of Fargo." *Reform Advocate* (Chicago), Dec. 13, 1913, special issue (photocopy). JHSUM.

"History of the Jews of Mesaba Range." *Reform Advocate* (Chicago), Oct. 25, 1913, special issue (photocopy). JHSUM.

"History of the Jews of Minneapolis and St. Paul." *Reform Advocate* (Chicago), Nov. 16, 1907, special issue. MHS.

Hosen, Freda. "South Dakota Jews Inherit Interesting History." *Sioux Falls* (S.Dak.) *Argus-Leader,* July 15, 1976, p. 16C.

Hyman, Paula [E]. "The Volunteer Organizations: Vanguard or Rear Guard?" *Lilith* (New York), no. 5 (1978): 16–17, 22.

"Jewish Organizations in St. Paul." *American Jewish World* (Minneapolis), Sept. 10, 1920, p. 72–73. JHSUM; MHS.

"Jewish Organizations of Minneapolis." *American Jewish World* (Minneapolis), Sept. 10, 1920, p. 79–81. JHSUM; MHS.

McWilliams, Carey. "Minneapolis: The Curious Twin." *Common Ground* (Autumn 1946): 61–65.

Nauen, Joyce. "They Came to Sioux Falls." *Jewish Chronicle* (London), Apr. 17, 1964, p. 9.

Pratt, Norma Fain. "Transitions in Judaism: The Jewish American Woman through the 1930s." *American Quarterly* 30 (Winter 1978): 681–702.

Schloff, Linda Mack. "Overcoming Geography: Jewish Religious Life in Four Market Towns." *Minnesota History* 51 (Spring 1988): 2–14.

*Thal, Sarah. As told to Martha Thal in "The Epic of Sarah Thal: Trail Blazer." *American Hebrew* (New York), Apr. 3, 1931, p. 531, 560-62. HUC-JIR.

*Wexler, Muriel. "Auxiliary President's Report." *Mount Sinai Hospital Messenger* (Minneapolis), Dec. 1976, p. 12. JHSUM; MHS.

Index

Picture Credits

Photography in this book was provided by the individuals and institutions below. Names of photographers, when known, appear in parentheses.

American Jewish Archives: 174
Bess Frisch: 32
Carol Berlin: 187
Deadwood Public Library (South Dakota): 134
Edith Edelman: 92 (bottom)
Isya Braginsky: 34
Judee Epstein: 168
Jewish Historical Society of the Upper Midwest: 2, 15, 42, 44, 49, 55, 62, 67, 68, 70, 72, 77, 78, 87, 89, 92 (top left, top right), 104, 112, 119, 120, 121, 122, 129, 130 (top and bottom), 138, 140, 141, 144. 149, 153, 156, 163, 166, 167, 169, 176, 178, 194, 195, 196, 198, 202, 203, 205, 212, 213, 215, 218, 220
Marilyn Chiat: 103
Minneapolis Jewish Family and Children's Service: 133
Minnesota Historical Society: 13 (Eric Mortenson), 20 (Phil Hutchens), 38, 45, 54, 64, 84, 91 (Eric Mortenson), 93, 94 (Eric Mortenson), 112 (Eric Mortenson), 123 (Eric Mortenson), 159, 164 (Eric Mortenson), 192 (Eric Mortenson), 201, 208 (Eric Mortenson)
Rabbi Stacy Offner: 172
Renell Silver: 47, 48
Violet Mekler: 128
Wisconsin State Historical Society: 160 (Whi [x3] 48270)
YIVO Institute for Jewish Research: 11, 12, 18, 27, 31

Maps by Mui D. Le and Alan J. Willis, University of Minnesota Cartography Laboratory, Minneapolis